Walking of Lakeland

Paul Buttle

Being a Guide to a Considered full week's Pedestrian Peregrination amongst the Major Mountains and Valleys in the County of Cumbria.

With many additional Suggestions as will make it of Practical use for a Sojourn of a longer Duration,

And much useful Information as to the availability of Sustenance, Accommodation and Transportation to obviate such Worries as the Wayfarer might otherwise have in this Quarter.

MCMXCVII

amadorn

To my father who took me on my first steps as
a walker and never reproached me for the
path I chose to take thereafter.

ISBN 0 9519345 1 1
© P. Buttle. 1997
Published by Amadorn, 18 Brewery Lane, Keswick, Cumbria.
Typeset by An t-Údar, 18 Greta Villas, Keswick, Cumbria.
Printed by Nuffield Press, Abingdon, Oxfordshire.

CONTENTS

Introduction	4
Map of the tour	10
Day 1	12
Day 2	30
Day 3	40
Day 4	52
Day 5	62
Day 6	72
Day 7	84
Extending the tour	94

INTRODUCTION

There is no doubt but that the finest way of exploring the Lake District is to do so on foot; and better still if that exploration has the feel of being a continuous progression through an evolving landscape. It is hoped the user of this guide will attain such a perception: a journey of exploration, revealing a good part of Lakeland's intricate beauty.

Such a walk, however, can only be achieved in optimum weather conditions, and because, unfortunately, such conditions do not always appertain in the Lake District I have also described a **Low Level** alternate route for when weather conditions are not so favourable, and given consequently the 'main route' the title **High Level**.

Although the guide is devised to suit someone with only a week to spend in Lakeland I have also sought to make it of use to anyone with a longer period of time at their disposal. To this end I have included a number of suggestions, which I've called **Extra Day Options**, as to what to do should you decide to spend two nights rather than one at each of the walk's intervening six stop over points, plus some rough notes on how the walk might be extended by a further day or two. Using these options the guide can be used as a basis for a tour lasting up to a fortnight.

In the end therefore the guide has become what I would call a schema: an aid, a planner which the walker can use to devise a route to suit his or herself. This result pleases me for I have not set out to establish a rigid course from which the user should never deviate. It might be that no two users of this guide will ever follow exactly the same route: I should be pleased if this turns out to be so.

Safety on the Fells

Though we venture on the fells for pleasure, in certain conditions they can be hazardous; you should therefore take with you the following items:

A Map

This is essential; the sketch maps in this guide are not sufficient. There are three types of Ordnance Survey maps that can be considered:

The 'One Inch' Tourist Map of the Lake District. Scale 1: 63,360.
This map covers the whole Lake District. One inch on the map represents a mile on the ground. Although for me this is the map's great virtue I now

find the present edition painful to look at. It is printed on thin paper, covered with purple splodges and even has other material printed on the back of it! But worst of all, and this is an act of pure desecration, the contours, horror of horrors, have been metricated! How many people are there who visualise distances in miles but heights in metres?

The Landranger Series Sheets 89, 90 and 96. Scale 1: 50,000
Although only a slightly larger scale than the 'One Inch' map these maps are surprisingly clearer. They are completely metricated – two centimetres on the map represents a single kilometre. Buying all three maps however is, of course, a more expensive option than buying just the 'One Inch' map.

Outdoor Leisure Map English Lakes : Scale 1: 25,500
There are four of these maps which cover the Lake District. They are incredibly detailed maps though they are of course a more expensive option than the previous two as well as being somewhat heavier to carry. There is one drawback to these maps however: rights of way are represented with bold green dashed lines which is fine when they represent footpaths which actually exist but not so fine when they don't. Sometimes, quite often in fact, there may not actually be a path following a right of way at all and this can lead to no little confusion. Be careful when using these maps to notice the very faint black dashed lines on them which represent actual existing paths. Sometimes these can be very distinct pathways and it is often these paths you should be following rather than the bolder green rights of way.

Compass, whistle, torch and survival bag

The above items should all be carried for reasons of safety: a whistle to attract attention should you be in difficulties – the distress signal is six blasts every sixty seconds; a torch in case you become benighted; a survival bag – a large body sized plastic bag – to get into to shelter from the elements should you be unable to move for some reason; and a compass for obvious reasons. Only the last of these items have I ever had cause to use and that just once, in white out conditions.

Additional Winter Equipment

An **ice axe** and if possible **crampons**. Of the two the ice axe is more essential, though because our winters have become so mild of late I've not really had to use one for some years. For walkers crampons are only essential on rare occasions; for me most of those rare occasions have been when I've deliberately chosen to tackle an icy covered surface which I could easily have avoided had I wanted.

What else to take

The best way to travel is as light as possible. Bearing this dictum in mind take only two sets of clothing with you: one set to don during the day and one set to wear in the evening if during the day your clothes have got soaked. Soaking clothes should be worn the next day no matter how damp they remain – if it's fine they soon dry out, if it's wet they just get wetter. That's the hardy way (and the unsociable way as well, as you are bound to end up smelling a bit) – if you are soft (or more socially fastidious) take three sets of clothing. Take a good waterproof, a stout pair of boots and, if you intend walking twixt the autumnal and spring equinoxes, a scarf and gloves. The fell tops are often a lot colder than the valleys even in summer so you should be prepared for cold and wet conditions. Take a towel, soap, toothpaste and toothbrush; a book maybe and a notebook and pen, but always be conscious of keeping your rucksack as light as possible.

The camping option

Finding accommodation can often be a great worry when travelling. This is not so when camping, which is one of its major advantages – a major disadvantage is the extra weight it burdens you with. If you are camping you will obviously need to carry a tent, a sleeping bag, a karrimat (or similar) and possibly cooking equipment. I say 'possibly' because I think it is quite feasible to complete this tour without carrying any cooking gear at all and relying instead on cafes and pubs on the way (which are listed in the guide's 'Places of Sustenance' notes). Free of the necessity of having to carry cooking gear and food rations your pack will be all the lighter – though it has to be said mornings without a fresh brew and perhaps only a bowl of muesli to munch on will not be as cheerful as they could be.

Should you use the 'wild' camp sites suggested in the guide – sites on the fells themselves – then you almost certainly will want to carry cooking gear. In theory to use such sites you should have the landowner's permission but camping on the unenclosed open fell is very much an accepted part of Lakeland life. To ensure that this acceptance continues it is beholden on you to leave on the ground after camping no more than the imprint of where you have lain the night before and not a scintilla of aught else.

Public transport

On a walking tour you should not have need to use public transport but a variety of circumstances might arise which could cause you to have to use it. In each day's description therefore I've made reference to the local transport services available. To find out the times of these services phone Cumbria County Council's Journey Planner on 01228 60 6000, which provides an excellent time table service; or for information on bus services only telephone Cumberland Motor Services on 01946 63 222.

Accommodation

Throughout this guide I've given an outline of the range of accommodation available in various locations. For more detailed information ring the nearest information centre to each of these places, such as Keswick, Windermere and Whitehaven. A full list of such centres is given in the phone directory under Tourist Information.

If it all becomes harder than you expected

Ideally I would like this guide to be used by first time comers to the Lake District but I have no doubt even following the Low Level Route options would have been beyond my capabilities on my first visit; but then I was not a very fit youth. Here briefly then is how to rapidly adapt the tour if you find the going harder than you thought it would be:-

Day 1	The shorter High Level option
Day 2	The Low Level option to Wythburn then bus to High Lodore via Keswick.
Day 3	The Low Level option concluding in Buttermere.
Day 4	The Low Level options to Wasdale
Day 5	Across Styhead Pass to Borrowdale
Day 6	The Low Level Route as far as Stake Pass and thence into Great Langdale and along the valley to Elterwater
Day 7	Elterwater to Ambleside

This would be a very truncated tour but still rewarding.

In conclusion

Even after the passing of thirty years and more I still have a clear memory of my first holiday in the Lake District; no subsequent visit in my opinion can ever replicate the magic of one's first exploration. Whatever route one takes or whatever fells one climbs one's first visit to Lakeland is always likely to be unforgettable. Is there therefore a need for such a guide as this? I am persuaded there is (obviously, otherwise it would not have been produced) for I am convinced the options I have set out in this guide are options unlikely to be chosen through mere serendipity or even careful study of the map. I have little doubt the suggestions I've made in this guide will enhance the enjoyment of a walking tour of Lakeland, more especially if it is a first time visit. I compare the tour to my own first tour of Lakeland and whilst it includes all the high points I made then it includes many more besides.

Since 1992, when my first idea for such a tour appeared in magazine form, at least three guides have been published offering a similar concept. Each of these guides, in my view however, seems to aim at encompassing as many fell tops as possible, whilst I have aspired more to give a broad insight into the varying quality of Lakeland's landscape – if my route is a tough one, which it is, the courses these other guides present seem impossibly tough.

For more than half my lifetime now, I have had the good fortune to live in the Lake District and I still marvel at its phenomenal beauty. After each full day on the fells I still also marvel that the fulfilment and enjoyment I have obtained should come from such a simple activity as walking – what need is there for wealth? I hope each user of this guide may come to think the same.

Ar gach maoilinn tá síocháin

January, 1997

Grains Gill

Map of the Tour

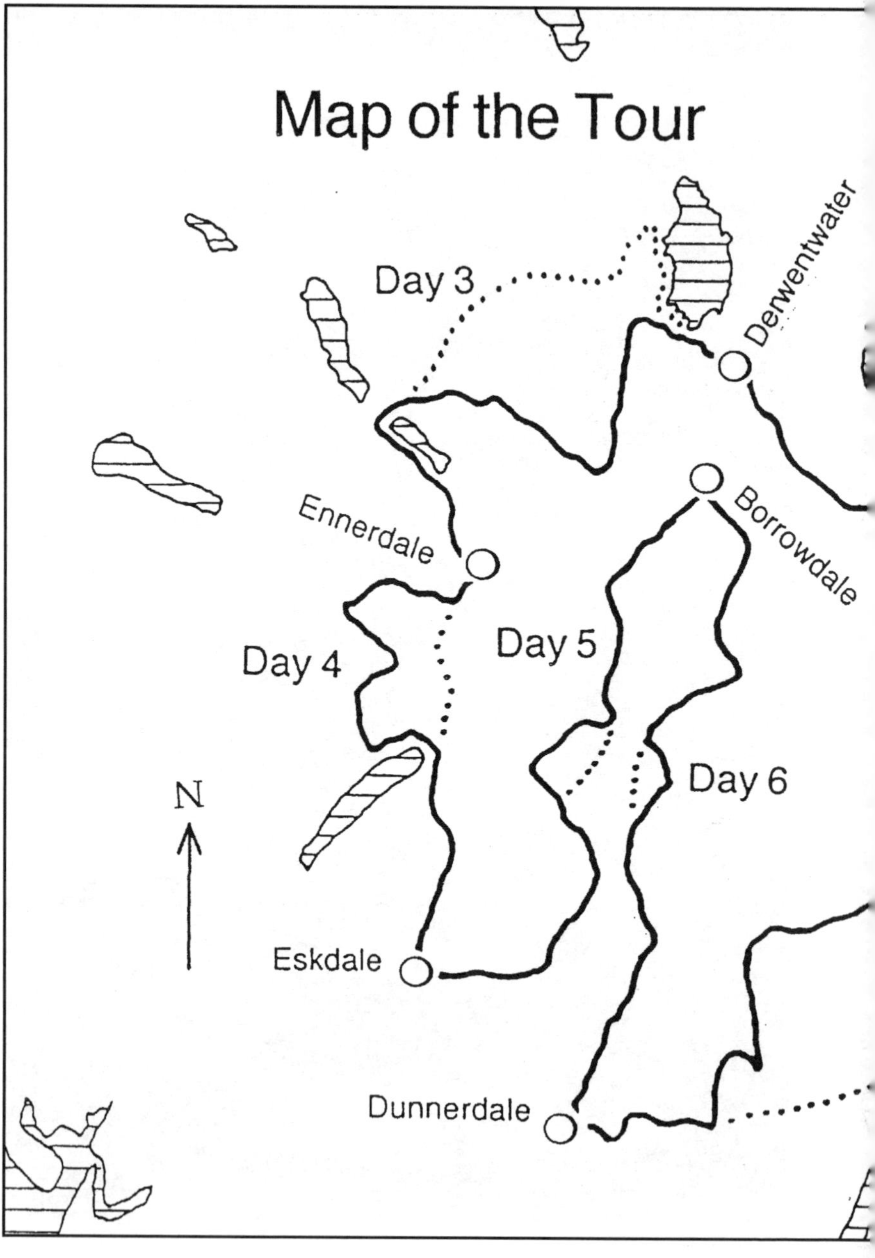

Day 3

Derwentwater

Ennerdale

Borrowdale

Day 4

Day 5

Day 6

N

Eskdale

Dunnerdale

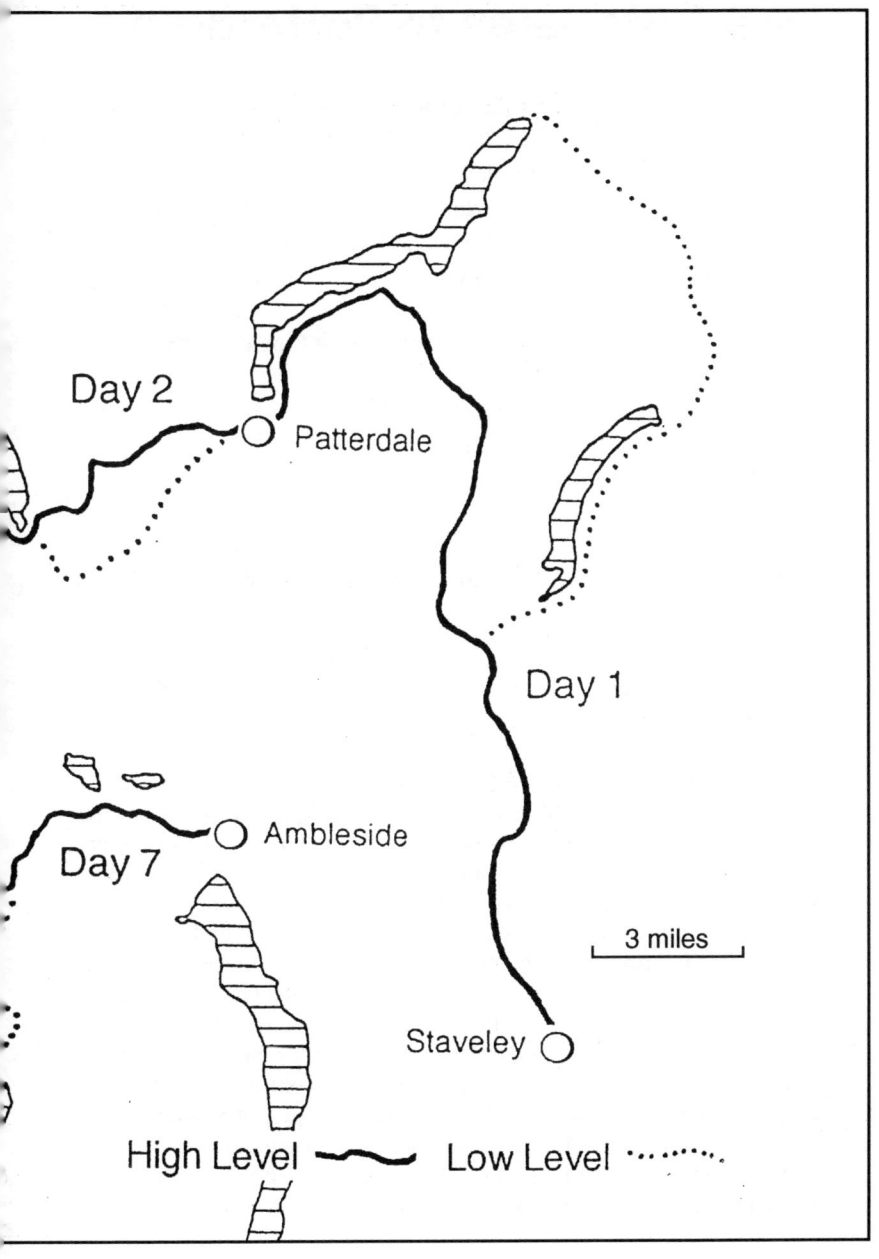

DAY 1 Staveley to Patterdale

	High Route	**Low Route**
Mileage	21 miles	23 miles
Total Feet of Ascent	3,500 feet	2,600 feet
Highest Point	High Street 2,719 feet	Nan Bield 2,200 feet
Suggested Time	11 hours	11 hours

	Shorter High Route Option
Mileage.	16 miles
Total Feet of Ascent	2,800 feet
Highest Point	High Street 2,719 feet
Suggested Time	8 hours
Starting Point	Staveley Railway Station (469 980)
Finishing Point	Patterdale Church (398 160)

DESCRIPTION

On this first day of the tour the High Level Route and Low Level Route are markedly different, though to begin with they follow the same course through the Kentmere valley: a wonderful dale in which one can often believe the last few centuries have failed to take place. At the head of the valley, however, at Nan Bield Pass, the high and low routes separate, the high route going on to breast the fell tops whilst the low route descends to Mardale where it continues along the solemn waters of the Haweswater reservoir eventually making its way to Pooley Bridge. The high route's chief object is the broad flat top of High Street, from which on a clear day to the west will be seen a wide range of fells which the tour passes through or over in the ensuing days. From High Street the route continues northwards eventually descending to Martindale, a valley the equal of Kentmere for peace and tranquillity, and finally concludes by following an undulating path along the shore line of Ullswater, the second largest lake in England, to Patterdale valley surrounded by an array of impressive fells.

LOGISTICS

High Level Route
This is a long day to begin with, much longer than I would really like it to be, though it can be accomplished. There are however three ways of shortening this first day if needs be. These are:-

1. Staying overnight in the village of Kentmere before starting on the tour in earnest. If you are only able to reach Staveley some time after mid-day this will be the only option open to you anyway. It is just under a five mile walk to Kentmere from Staveley, which can easily be accomplished in two or three hours. Such an afternoon or evening saunter, especially after some hours of travel, would serve both as a pleasing way to unwind and as a wonderful entrée into the tour ahead. Kentmere in any case is a far more congenial place to stay than Staveley. This option then would reduce the first day's mileage to a more manageable sixteen miles.

2. Using the Ullswater 'motor yacht' to sail from Howtown, which is a mile north-east of Martindale old church, to Glenridding Pier which in turn is a mile north of Patterdale. This reduces the day's mileage by approximately 3 miles – but a hard three miles along the shoreline of Ullswater. The service operates during he tourist season, usually from Easter to the end of October. (See page 7)

3. Descending directly from High Street to Patterdale via Angle Tarn, which shortens the first day's mileage by almost six miles, but at the expense of viewing the beauty of Martindale which undoubtedly would detract from the completeness of the tour. But if time is a-winging this is a useful option to bear in mind.

Low Level Route
This option should be avoided if at all possible, unless it is only intended to be done in part (see the next paragraph). It includes a lot of road walking and to my mind also involves moving out of the real Lake District even though the route stays within the boundary of the national park. I have included it because I recognise that the weather in the Lake District is not always perfect and in bad weather the high route would be a tough one to accomplish: so an alternative has to be offered.

The Low Level Route does though have one advantage – it affords the walker a better appreciation of the Mardale valley which contains the Haweswater reservoir: a striking valley with its own distinctive atmosphere. If therefore you have the time to extend the tour by a further day consider making Haweswater the object of your first day's journey rather than Patterdale. You can journey to Patterdale the day after either by continuing on the Low Level Route or, better still, climbing up to High Street and concluding the first day's High Level Route. How this latter option might be accomplished is suggested on page 25.

PUBLIC TRANSPORT (See also page 7)

Public transport connections between Staveley and Patterdale are not good. Whilst there are both rail and bus connections from Staveley to Windermere the bus connections between Windermere and Patterdale are very limited and at the time of writing only operate for a short period in the summer.

Two other services relevant to this section of the walk are a bus service that runs from Staveley to Kentmere and the Ullswater 'motor yacht'. The bus service is a recent limited summer service begun in 1994: hopefully it will still be operating when you read these words. The 'motor yacht' has been operating for over 100 years and connects Pooley Bridge Pier (464 243) with Howtown Pier (442 199) and Glenridding Pier (390 169) usually from Easter to October.

ACCOMMODATION (See also page 7)

Staveley Three inns and a number of guest houses.

Kentmere Limited, no more than one or two guest houses.

Martindale A limited number of guest houses and the Howtown Hotel.

Patterdale Patterdale Hotel, several guest houses and a Youth Hostel.

Haweswater The Haweswater Hotel. Bunkhouse accommodation may also be provided by new owner of the hotel in future years.

Pooley Bridge Two inns and about half a dozen guest houses.

CAMPING

The only official camping site on the main route is Side Farm in Patterdale

(396 167). In the past, however, I have found one or two farmers have allowed me to camp in their fields in Kentmere and perhaps the same might apply for Martindale. It is also possible to camp in Mardale although there is no official campsite there.

PLACES OF SUSTENANCE

Staveley Three pubs, two of which serve bar meals. Also a small craft shop serves light refreshments through the day.

Kentmere Maggs Howe Farm in Kentmere's Green Quarter serves light refreshments throughout the day.

Howtown The Howtown Hotel serves teas. There is also a small public bar at the back of the hotel.

Patterdale The Patterdale Hotel and the White Lion both serve bar meals and breakfasts even, the former though 'only if we have space'.

Haweswater The Haweswater Hotel serves bar meals and other refreshments throughout the day.

Pooley Bridge The village has three pubs which serve bar meals and two small cafes.

SHOPS

Staveley Good village stores.

Patterdale Post Office: a well provisioned shop also selling newspapers.

Pooley Bridge Village store.

EXTRA DAY OPTIONS

Patterdale is where I spent my first 'rest day' in the Lake District, and I can make no better suggestion as to what to do on such a day in Patterdale as that which I did then: a wander over Place Fell (40 16). It is a modest fell and usually fairly quiet. Should you not be intending to tackle the following day's High Level Route you could also consider tackling Helvellyn unencumbered with baggage, though this would rob the following day of its freshness somewhat.

DAY 1 Staveley to Patterdale

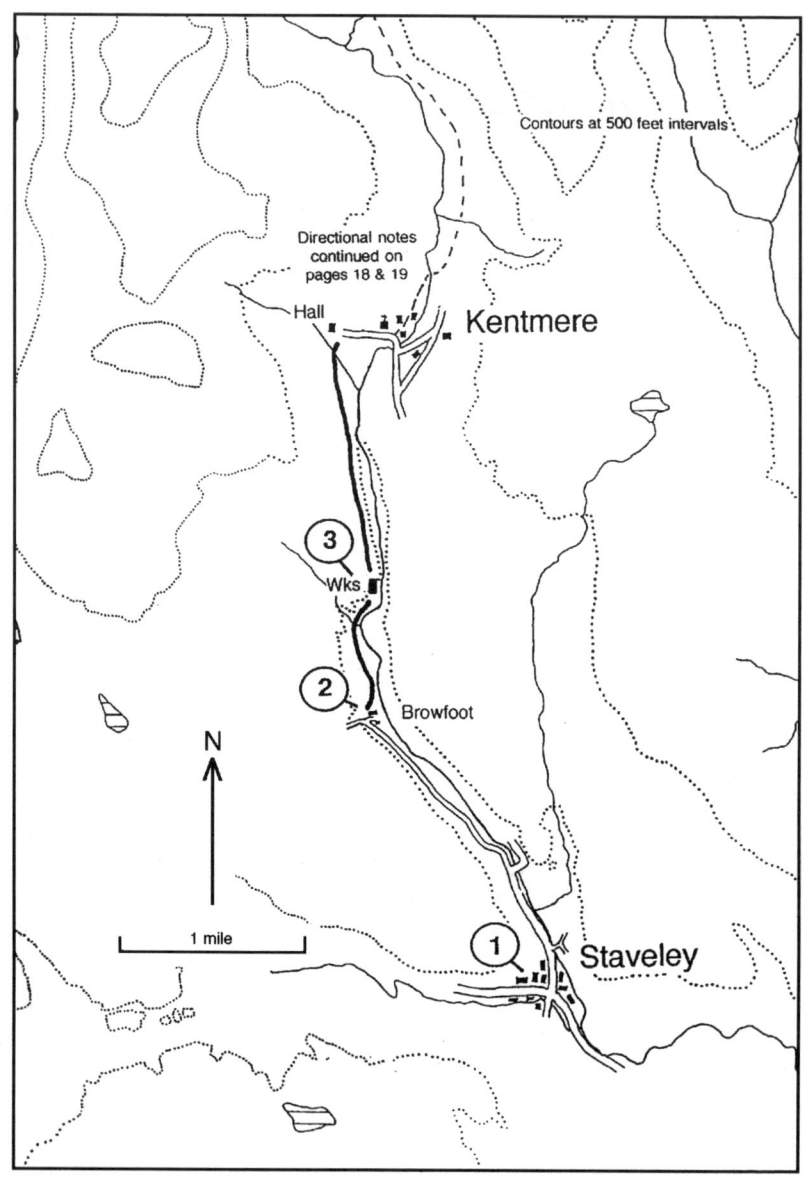

High Level Route

1. After descending the steps from Staveley railway station turn left along Station Road. Within a few hundred yards it joins the main road running through the village. Cross over the road and follow the road sign-posted as leading to Kentmere. Just over half a mile from the village the valley road to Kentmere village swings right across a bridge spanning the Kent river. Here continue straight ahead on a narrower road keeping to the west of the river and signposted as leading to Browfoot. After passing Browfoot Farm notice to your right a sign with the words "Cyclists Please Dismount Before Entering the Farmyard" at the start of a rough trackway. (2 miles)

2. The trackway is a right of way which leads between the farm and its outbuildings and then parallels the river. (A more prominently signed concessionary path skirts around Browfoot Farm but at the time of writing it would seem the wayfarer still has the right to pass through the farmyard.) A quarter mile from the farm the trackway comes to a narrow surfaced lane. Here turn left. Passing between two opulent domiciles the lane becomes a rough trackway. About a hundred yards further on an enclosed trackway leads off to the right which in turn leads to an enclosed footpath which, after crossing a small footbridge, leads to the driveway of a tall white house. Continue along this driveway till you come to, of all things, a small factory! (1 mile)

3. Continue through the factory yard (it is a right of way even if there is a barrier barring the way – this is to prevent vehicles not walkers). At the far end of the yard the route continues initially as a concrete lane and then as a broad pathway. About a mile along this path another broad path cuts across it. Here turn right and follow the new pathway to Kentmere Hall. (1 ½ miles)

DAY 1 Staveley to Patterdale

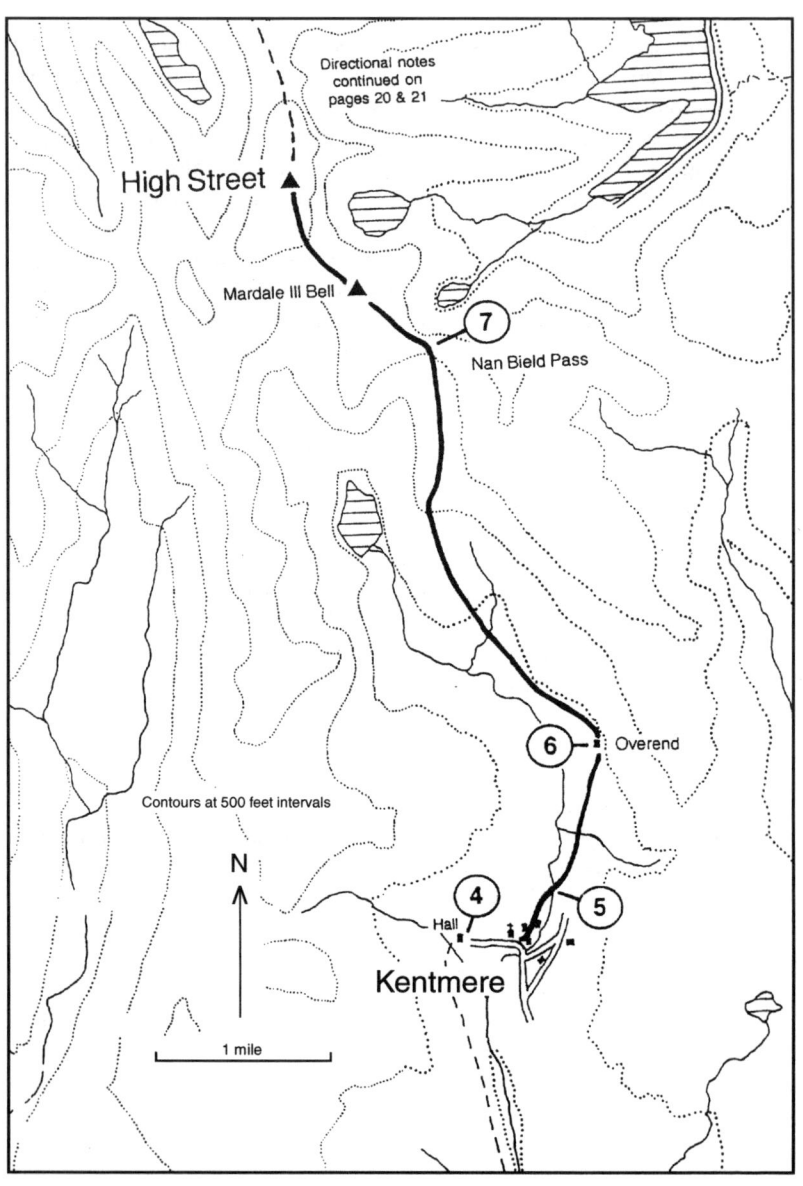

High Level Route

4   From the Hall follow the farm's access road to Kentmere church where you come to a surfaced road. Here turn right and within fifty yards turn left on to a roadway passing the gable end of the church and signposted rather oddly as being a public footpath to Upper Kentmere and Kentmere Reservoir. Less than a hundred yards along this road branch right on to a rough enclosed trackway. Approximately two hundred yards after passing through Rook Howe farmyard the trackway nears the river Kent, spanning which is a prominent wooden footbridge. Beginning from a narrow gap in the right-hand enclosing wall of the trackway a path leads to this footbridge, on the other side of which it branches in two. (¾ mile)

5   Follow the left-hand branch which pulls up to a high stone wall in which is set a stile. On the other side of the wall is to be discovered an enclosed trackway. Here turn left. Where the trackway becomes unenclosed and crosses a swift flowing beck it branches in two. Follow the left-hand branch. Where the track swings right to climb up to Hallow Bank be careful to branch left on to another trackway that leads to the hamlet of Overend where the valley's surfaced roadway terminates. (¾ mile)

6   Here a very small wooden signpost, only a few feet high, points to a much grassier trackway branching off to the right, indicating that it is a 'Bridleway to Mardale and Nan Bield Pass'. Initially, though none too visibly to begin with, the right of way follows the outer side of the wall to your left. Once having crossed a small stream however the bridleway is quite distinct and there is little difficulty following it here on to the top of Nan Bield Pass. (2 ¾ miles)

7   At the top of the pass turn left and follow a distinct path to the top of Mardale Ill Bell. From this summit the path continues on to the High Street ridge along the crest of which runs a dilapidated wall. On reaching the wall follow its course uphill to the summit of High Street which is marked with a large trig point. (1 ¼ miles)

DAY 1 Staveley to Patterdale

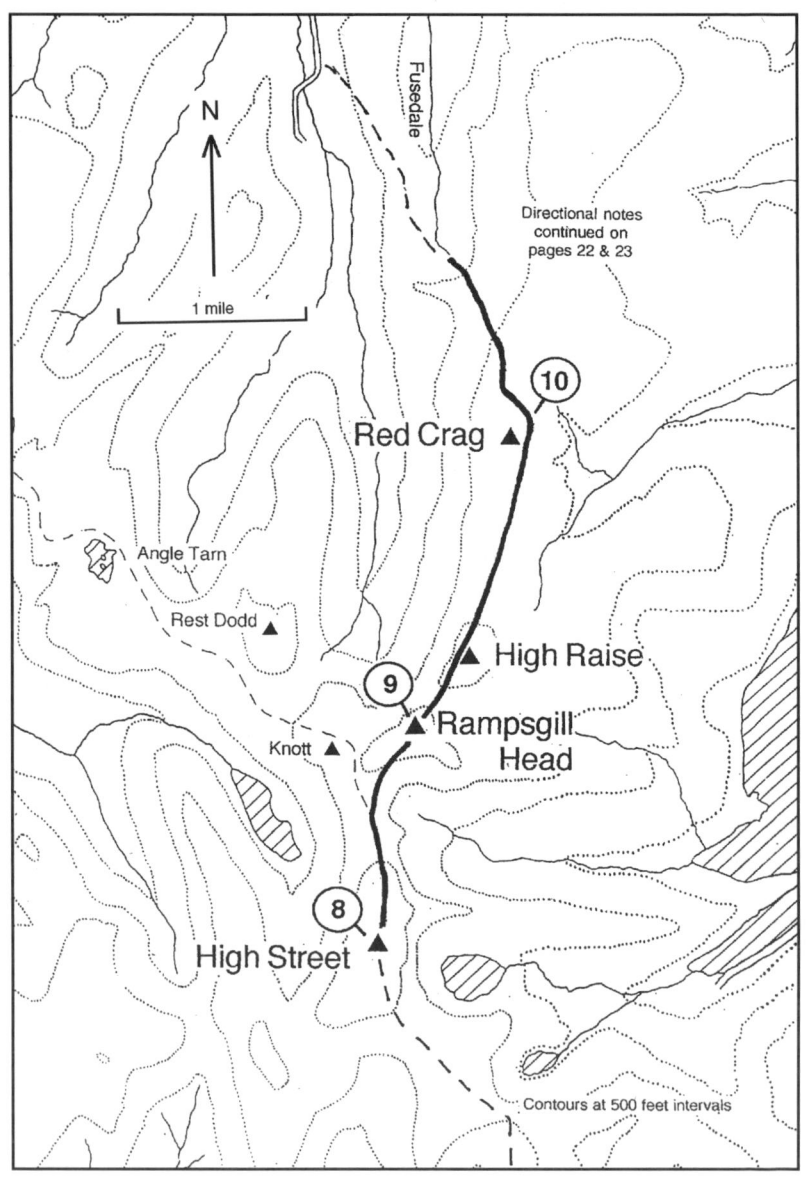

High Level Route

(If at this point you are feeling tired or are running out of daylight there is a quicker route to Patterdale as mentioned in the logistic notes. To use this route from the summit of High Street follow the stone wall northwards to a small gap between The Knott and Rampsgill Head. Here a path moves round The Knott and begins to descend in a north-westerly direction. After 300 feet of descent the path splits in two, though you may hardly notice this as the right-hand branch is much bolder. Continue along the bolder, right-hand path which traverses the lower slopes of Rest Dodd and finally arrives at Angle Tarn. Here the path continues around the northern end of the tarn and then leads to Boardale Hause where it then descends directly to Patterdale. Otherwise if you are still bursting with energy the more complete route is as follows:)

8   From the top of High Street follow the wall northwards to the Straits of Riggindale, the gap between High Street and Rampsgill Head. As it climbs uphill again notice about a hundred yards from the start of the climb a very broad path veering off to the right. A quarter of a mile along this path another path veers off to the left to the top of Rampsgill Head; it is, however, so inconspicuous you are likely to miss it, in which case when the path you are on seems to be swinging distinctly right and has become fairly level strike out to your left. This way you will, hopefully, either discover the cairns atop of Rampsgill Head or the correct path leading to it. (1 ¼ miles)

9   From Rampsgill Head continue in a north-easterly direction. There is no clear path to begin with but within a hundred yards or so one becomes obvious. The path passes a little to the west of High Raise, the range's next top, and a few hundred yards afterwards it begins following a wire fence. Crossing over Red Crag, the very inauspicious rise in the ridge after High Raise, the main path veers away from the fence to the right. At this point however keep to the line of the fence. A little more than half a mile further on the fence comes close to a dilapidated wall. (2 ¼ miles)

10 A path leads from the fence to a currently gateless gap in the ruined wall from which it continues diagonally down the fell side to the head of Fusedale where there stands an isolated ruin. (¾ mile)

DAY 1 Staveley to Patterdale

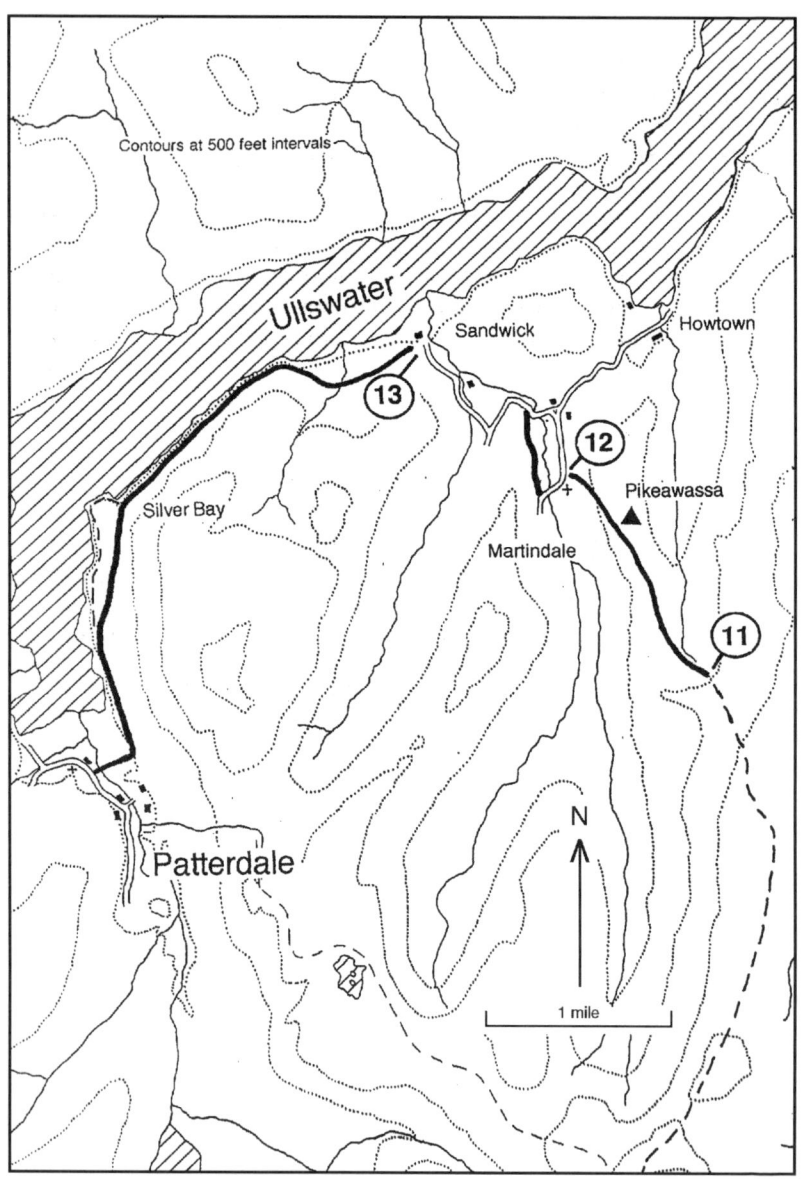

High Level Route

11 From the ruin follow a path which leads from its gable end across the beck flowing past it. This path leads around the head of Fusedale and climbs uphill slightly to curve round the side of Brownthwaite Crag, where it then descends diagonally across the fellside of Pikeawassa to the old church of St. Martin's in Martindale. (1 ¼ mile)

12 From St Martin's church follow the road south-eastwards to a stone bridge. A hundred yards or so past the bridge is the start of a bridleway leading off to the right behind Winter Crag Farm which in the space of half a mile comes to another roadway. Here turn left. Where the road comes to a junction turn right and follow the road to Sandwick. Just before reaching the hamlet, a few hundred yards from the lakeshore of Ullswater, an isolated three pointer signpost indicates a bridleway leading off to the left. (1 ½ miles)

13 This path follows the lakeshore of Ullswater to Patterdale. At Silver Bay the path branches in two – the higher path has better views but at this stage of the walk you may not have the energy to take it even though it requires only a small degree of climbing to accomplish. Reaching the end of the lake the path becomes a broad trackway leading to Side Farm. On reaching the farm turn right into the farm and follow the farm's access road to the main A592. Patterdale Church is a few yards to the right whilst the Post Office, hotel and youth hostel are within half a mile to the left. (4 miles)

DAY 1 Staveley to Patterdale

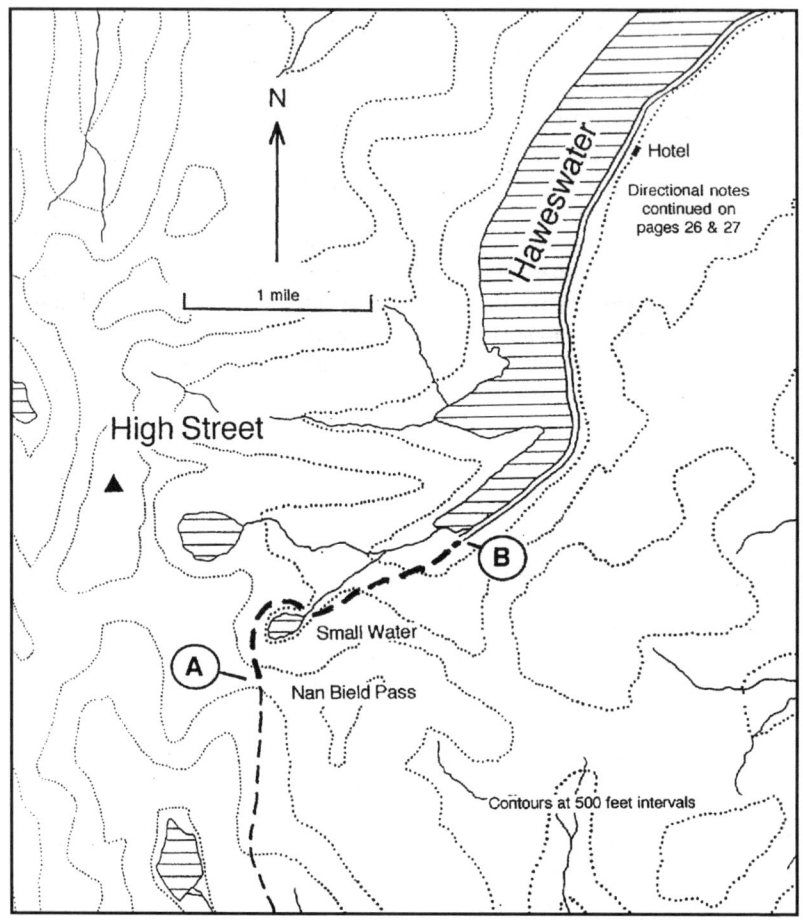

Follow the High Level Route to Nan Bield Pass (pages 16 to 19 up to directional note 6) and then continue as follows:-

A On reaching Nan Bield Pass descend the old, carefully zig-zagged packhorse route on the other side to the small tarn of Small Water and beyond to the head of Haweswater Reservoir where the path joins a car park sited at the terminus of the Haweswater road. (1 ½ miles)

Low Level Route

B The easiest way to the Haweswater Hotel is to follow the road, but there is also a path covering the same distance existing between the road and the reservoir. It begins at the car park's exit, from a small, unsigned, gap in the wall. There is no sign of a path to begin with: simply follow the base of the road's retaining wall. Within a few hundred yards something akin to a sheep trod develops, after which there seems to be definite signs of the path's construction. You are in fact following a seemingly defunct pipe line. After reaching the reservoir's straining tower it is best at this point to rejoin the road; though a path does continue along the base of the road's retaining wall it is not very appealing. Should you choose to follow it, however, notice half a mile from the tower a large square building up to your right: the garages of the Haweswater Hotel. Ten yards past the garages is a gap in the road's retaining wall giving access to both the road and the hotel. (2 ¼ miles)

(As suggested in the Logistic notes, if you have the time, a better option to continuing on the Low Level Route at this point would be to stay overnight in the valley and then rejoin the first day's High Level Route by climbing up to High Street the following day. To do this:

Return to the car park at the terminus of the Haweswater road and continue on the path climbing up to Small Water. Less than a hundred yards from the car park turn right on to a signposted path for Brampton. This distinct path goes round the end of the reservoir and climbs uphill slightly to the crest of a ridge the final part of which projects in to the waters of the reservoir.

At the crest of this ridge, after passing through a dilapidated wall, notice a narrower path leading off to the left following the line of the ridge. The path follows this ridge to the top of High Street. On gaining the rim of High Street's broad summit top however the line of the path becomes less than evident. Here you should in fact veer left; one isolated cairn marks the correct direction to take. On reaching a long ruinous wall follow it southwards to a large white trig point which marks the summit of High Street.

If you do not have the time to stay in the valley continue on to the next page....)

DAY 1 Staveley to Patterdale

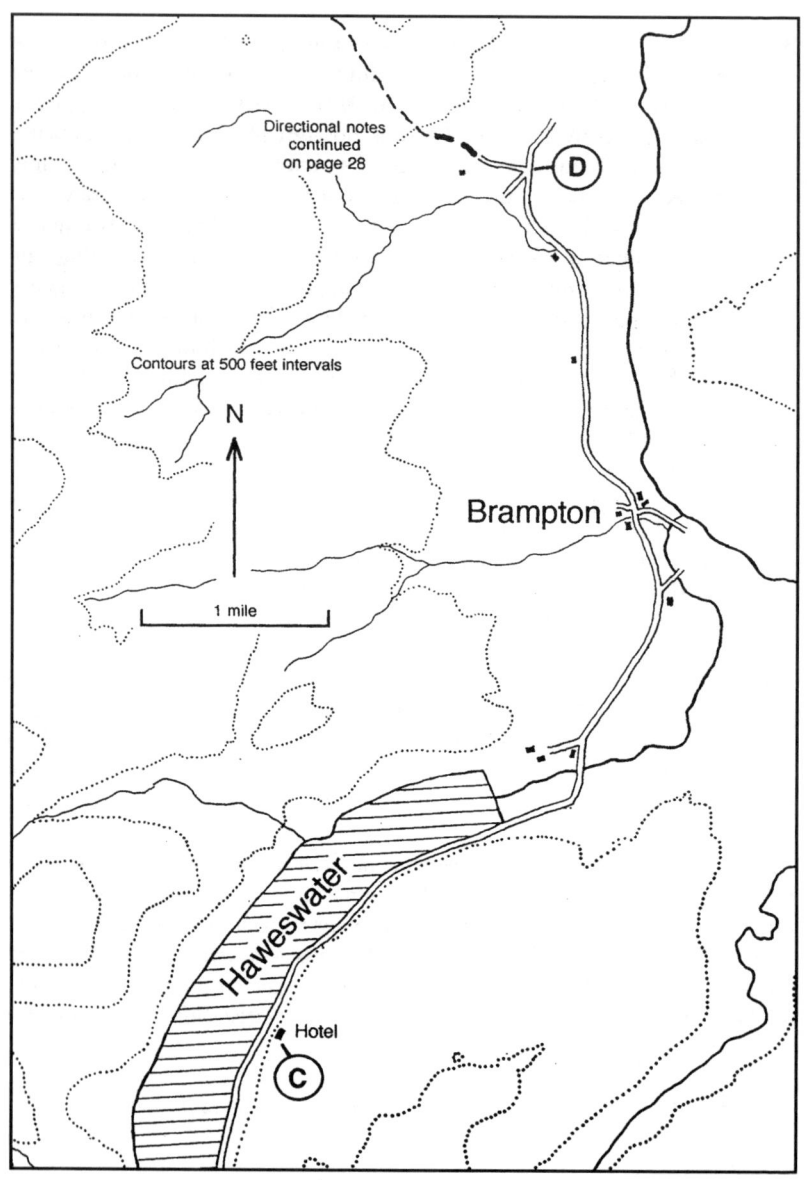

Low Level Route

C   From the hotel follow the road north-eastwards. (Between the road and the reservoir is a permissive path marked red on the 25,000 OS maps. Access down to it from the hotel is gained through a small stile on the left-hand side of the road just north of the hotel's garages. This path parallels the road for about a mile and a half but is so narrow and undulating it is debatable as to whether there is much advantage in using it unless the road is particularly busy.) Once past the dam follow the road signs for Penrith. Roughly two miles past the village of Brampton, just before coming to the village sign for Helton, leading off to the left, past a stone barn, is a road which leads to Widewath Farm. (5 ¾ miles)

D   A wooden signpost pointing to the road indicates that it is a public bridleway. Where the surfaced road swings left to Widewath Farm the bridleway continues straight ahead along an enclosed trackway. After passing through a metal gate the way becomes a confusion of tracks, but by walking straight forward a wooden signpost soon comes into view a couple of hundred yards ahead. (½ mile)

DAY 1 Staveley to Patterdale

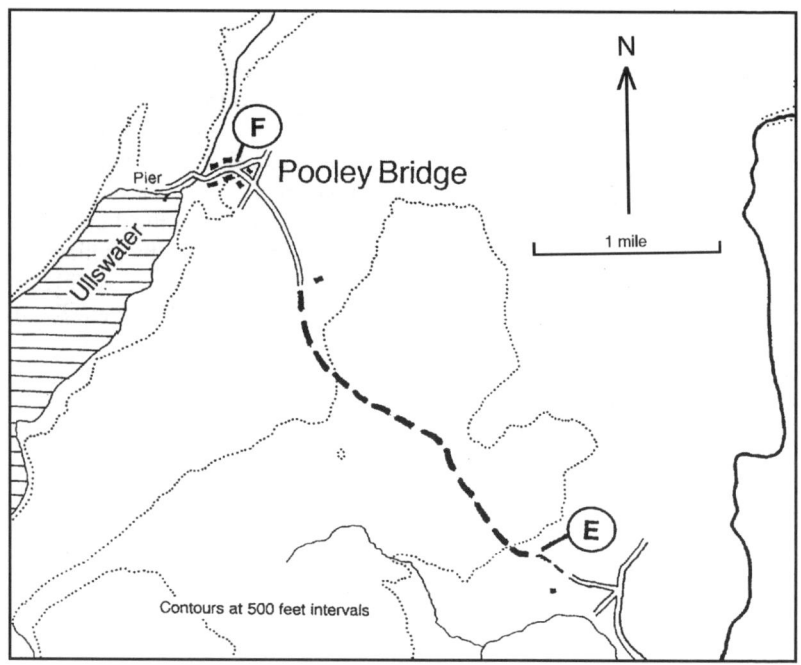

E   The sign points to a trackway indicated as being a bridleway to Howtown and Pooley Bridge. About a mile along the track another trackway cuts across it. Here simply continue walking straight ahead as another nearby signpost indicates you should do to reach Pooley Bridge. Eventually the track merges into a tarmacadamed road which leads directly to Pooley Bridge village. (2 ¾ miles)

F   On reaching the main road through the village turn left and pass through the village and a quarter mile further on reach Pooley Bridge Pier. From the pier, between Easter to October, it is possible to utilise the Ullswater 'motor yacht' to reach the Glenridding Pier at the southern end of the lake sited a mile north of Patterdale village. (1 ½ miles) *(Or alternatively utilise the Penrith to Patterdale bus which picks up passengers from the centre of the village.)*

Ullswater

DAY 2 Patterdale to Derwentwater

	High Route	**Low Route**
Mileage	13 miles	12 ½ miles
Total Feet of Ascent	3,900 feet	2,600 feet
Highest Point	Helvellyn	Seat Sandal Col
	3,116 feet	1,850 feet
Suggested Time	9 hours	7 hours
Starting Point	Patterdale Church (398 158)	
Finishing Point	High Lodore Farm (261 183)	

DESCRIPTION

The High Level Route tackles the third highest summit in the Lake District: Helvellyn. Although Scafell and Scafell Pike are slightly higher, Helvellyn is reckoned to be the most visited mountain top in Cumbria, probably due to it being somewhat more accessible than the two higher peaks. The ascent route follows Striding Edge the most impressive arête in the Lake District. This is the most dramatic and difficult route to the top but paradoxically, because of these qualities, it has also become the most popular way to the summit.

The Low Level Route parallels the higher route by following the length of the Grisedale valley. This is a very impressive valley with some massive crags towering over it, making this route almost as dramatic as the higher one.

Both routes link up at the top end of Thirlmere and the day concludes with a crossing of the ridge which lies between Thirlmere and Derwentwater – one of the soggiest stretches of land in the Lake District. The crossing however is rewarded by a visit to the hamlet of Watendlath sited in its own narrow valley next to the tarn named after it – an idyllic setting. From the hamlet following the Watendlath valley northwards a much wider valley is reached containing the broad waters of Derwentwater overlooked by the massive shape of Skiddaw formed of the oldest rocks in Lakeland.

LOGISTICS

If desired the day's walking can be substantially shortened by using public transport, this being so these details are best left to the next section.

PUBLIC TRANSPORT (See also page 7)

On reaching the A591 a bus to Keswick can be hailed either from the top of Dunmail Raise (326 116) or opposite Wythburn Church (324 137) (a phone box next to the church enables you to enquire of the time of the next bus). Then from Keswick you can use the Borrowdale bus to reach the southern end of Derwentwater. This avoids having to make a thousand foot plus ascent – a bit daunting if you've already crossed over Helvellyn – and some miles of tramping through virtual bog. On the other hand it does negate the purity of the tour being accomplished solely on foot and it would also involve getting embroiled in the commercialisation of Keswick and the aimless hordes that mill around there – no matter how much you strain to avert your gaze. Better then to face up to the day's final climb and the squelching bogland that lies twixt Wythburn and Watendlath.

If for any reason you are not up to walking any of this day's mileage there are good public transport connections between Patterdale and the southern end of Derwentwater but this usually involves travelling via Penrith, a long and not particularly attractive journey for the most part: bus from Patterdale to Penrith, then bus from Penrith to Keswick and finally a third bus (the Borrowdale bus which follows the B5289) to the southern end of the lake; or alternatively you can use the Derwentwater launch which from the boat landings in Keswick (264 226) calls at the Ashness boat landings (269 202) and the Lodore boat landings (264 192). During the school summer holidays this journey can be shortened by using a bus service which then operates directly between Patterdale and Keswick.

ACCOMMODATION (See also page 7)

B&Bs and Guest Houses At Watendlath (275 163), Ashness (270 192), and High Lodore (260 182).

Hotels Borrowdale Hotel (260 181) and the Lodore Hotel (263 189)

Youth Hostel Barrow House (269 200) a fine Georgian house overlooking Derwentwater.

CAMPING

Ashness Farm (270 192) is the only official camping site on this day's route. A good 'wild' camping site would be the area around Blea Tarn.

PLACES OF SUSTENANCE

Watendlath Over many years the forecourt to one of the farmhouses in this hamlet has developed into a very popular tea garden – closed in winter.

High Lodore A small, basic, cafe is situated in the outbuilding of High Lodore Farm, offering perhaps the most inexpensive fare in the Lake District – closed in winter. More up-market both the Borrowdale Hotel (260 181) and the Lodore Hotel (263 189) serve teas and meals to non-residents.

Grange This small hamlet (252 170) has no less than two cafes – one of which at the time of writing is attempting to keep open throughout the year.

SHOPS

Patterdale P.O. This is the best shopping opportunity for food for the next two days, unless that is you are prepared to divert off course to visit Keswick.

EXTRA DAY OPTIONS

A leisurely option would be to consider boating on Derwentwater. The more energetic option would be to make an ascent of Skiddaw unencumbered with luggage. Do this by first bussing in to Keswick. There is a route from the town to the summit known as the 'Tourist Route', but better still would be to take a further bus to High Side Farm (234 306) five miles to the north-west of Keswick and then ascend Skiddaw via Ullock Pike (243 289) using the 'Tourist Route' as your descent route back to Keswick.

Striding Edge

DAY 2 Patterdale to Derwentwater

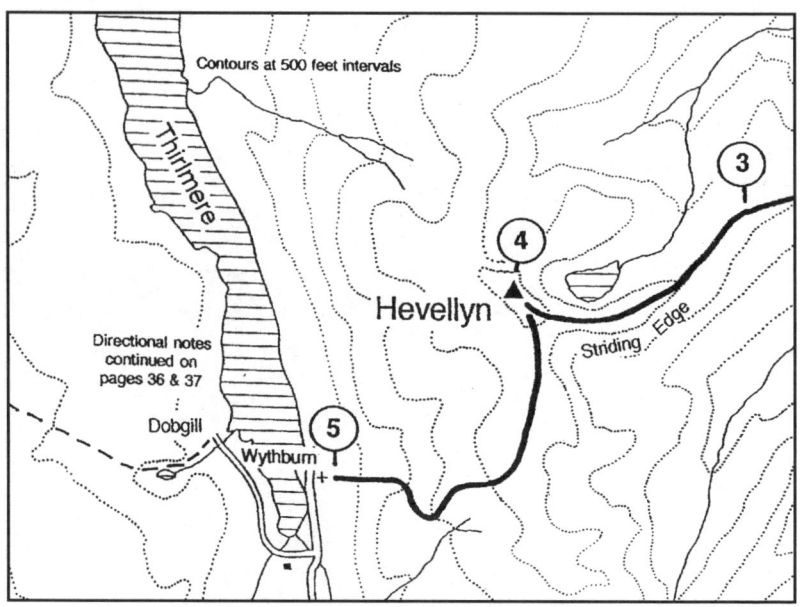

1   From Patterdale church follow the main A592 westwards. About three hundred yards from the church take the first turn left on to an unsigned surfaced road. The road soon swings right and climbs uphill a little and eventually comes to a six bar gate. (¾ mile)

2   Here a narrower access road to Grassthwaite Howe strikes off to the right, a wooden sign indicating that it is also a 'footpath' to Helvellyn. Where the access road makes a sharp turn right continue directly ahead through a kissing gate giving access to a steep worn path leading straight uphill to a second kissing gate. Pass through this second gate and turn left. The path immediately branches in two. Take the right-hand steeper, broader option. After a long steep climb the path reaches a stone wall in which is sited a wooden stile. (1 ½ miles)

3   Cross over the stile and follow the path leading along the ridge ahead of you which develops into Striding Edge proper. Outside of the winter season there is no great difficulty to this ridge; the most

High Level Route

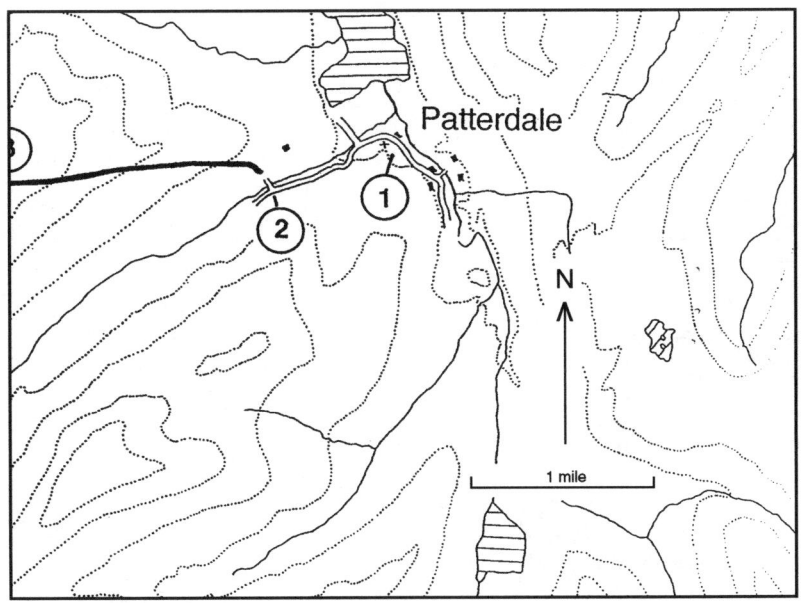

exciting way of crossing it is to keep to the crest of the ridge as much as possible. If needed however there is a much easier, though narrower, path that can be used just below the crest of the ridge on its right-hand side. On reaching the summit ridge turn right and walk the last few remaining hundred yards to the summit trig point. (1 ¼ miles)

4   From the trig point walk southwards along a broad pathway. About half a mile from the summit the path splits in two. Take the right-hand lower path which makes a long steep descent to Wythburn Church. (2 ¼ miles)

5   From the church follow the trackway leading from the church's car park. Just before reaching the roadway pass through a kissing gate on the left-hand side of the track on to a pathway signposted as leading to Grasmere and follow it as far as a second signpost where the main road forms a junction with another road leading to Armboth. Follow the Armboth road as far as Dobgill Car Park. (1 ½ miles)

DAY 2 Patterdale to Derwentwater

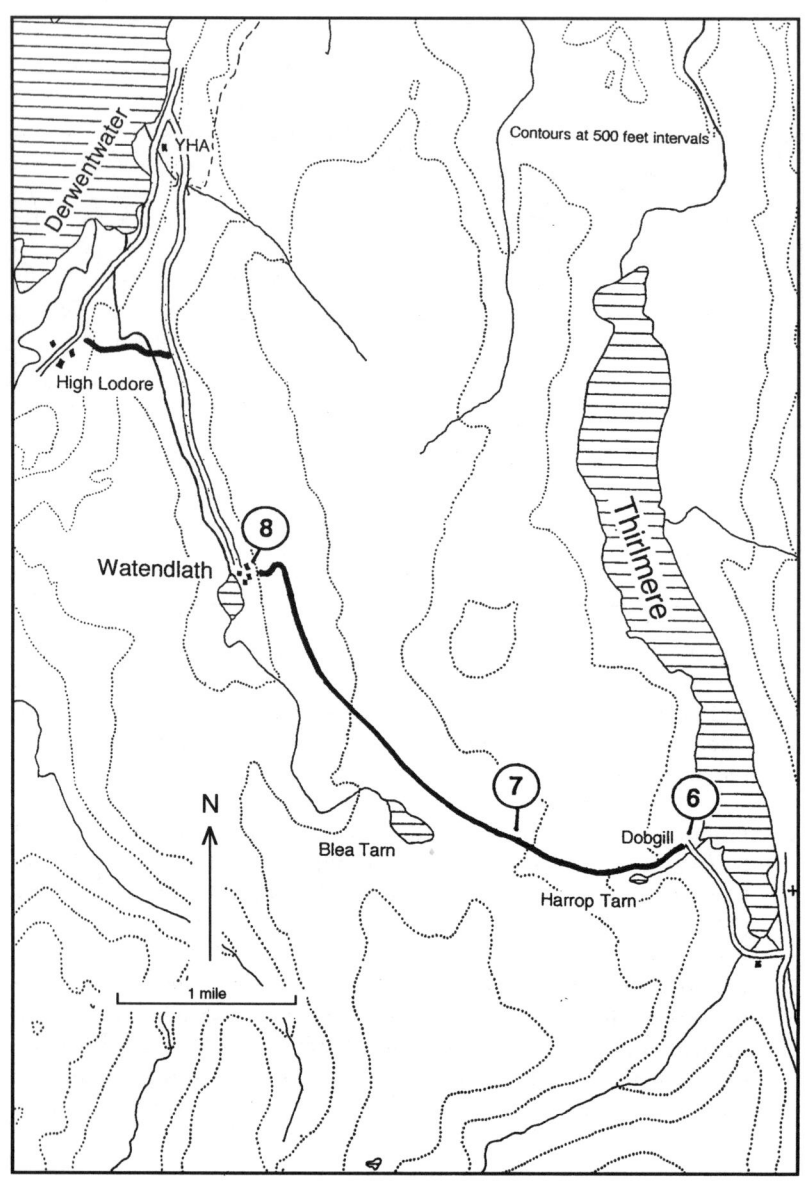

High Level Route

6 From the corner of the car park is a gate giving access to a path leading to Harrop Tarn. On reaching Harrop Tarn the path joins a broad trackway. Here turn right and follow the trackway. Where this swings right away from Mosshause Gill, the beck that feeds into the tarn, a signpost indicates a public bridleway which continues to follow the side of Mosshause Gill and which soon links up with another forestry track. A hundred yards or so along this track, indicated by nothing more than a blue arrow way mark, a narrow path branches off to the right. In little more than half a mile this path breaks out of the forest and leads to the top of the ridge separating Thirlmere from Watendlath along which runs a wire fence. (1 ¼ miles)

7 There now follows one of the soggiest paths in the Lake District with little more to follow than the crushed appearance of the mosses and rushes which most other people have followed before. Drawing near the outflow of Blea Tarn the path veers right and climbs a little uphill. At this point two or three cairns indicate the actual course of the route and from here on the route is more discernible though hardly drier. On reaching a small copse of fir trees the path turns left. Acquiring a cobbled surface it then descends to the homely hamlet of Watendlath. (2 ¼ miles)

8 Follow the road leading northwards from the hamlet. *(If you are aiming to reach the Derwentwater youth hostel follow the road for just over two miles to a point a few hundred yards past Ashness Bridge. Here look for a small gate in the left-hand side wall which gives access to a private path leading directly to the youth hostel. Otherwise...)* Continue along the road for just over a mile to an isolated barn. Just past the barn, just before coming to a cattle grid, a wooden sign indicates the start of a public footpath to High Lodore and Borrowdale beginning from a wooden stile on the left-hand side of the road. The path leads down to a footbridge spanning Watendlath Beck. On the other side of the bridge is a worn path roughly following the course of the river. Here turn right. Within about 100 yards the path splits in two: bear left. The path leads down to High Lodore Farm situated on the B 5289. (1 ¾ miles)

DAY 2 Patterdale to Derwentwater

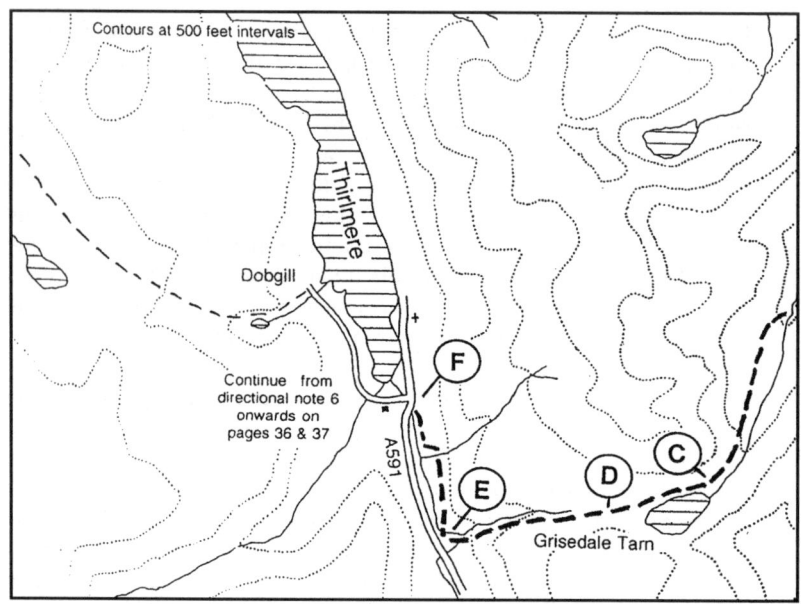

A   Walking westwards from Patterdale church take the first turn left on to an unsigned surfaced road. The road soon swings right and climbs uphill a little and eventually comes to a six bar gate. (¾ mile)

B   Here a narrower tarmacadamed access road strikes off to the right. Ignore this turning and continue pressing forward on the surfaced roadway. The road soon becomes a rough trackway and after passing Elmhow it reduces to a bridleway. After a long steady of climb of a thousand feet the path comes to a large cairn at which point Grisedale Tarn comes into view. (3 miles)

C   Here the path branches in two. Continue along the right-hand branch. After a hundred yards or so a thinner, boggier, path branches off to the left roughly contouring round the northern side of Grisedale Tarn. Where this path curves to the left notice a path branching off to the right, towards an isolated metal post, across the lowest point twixt Dollywaggon Pike and Seat Sandal. (½ mile)

Low Level Route

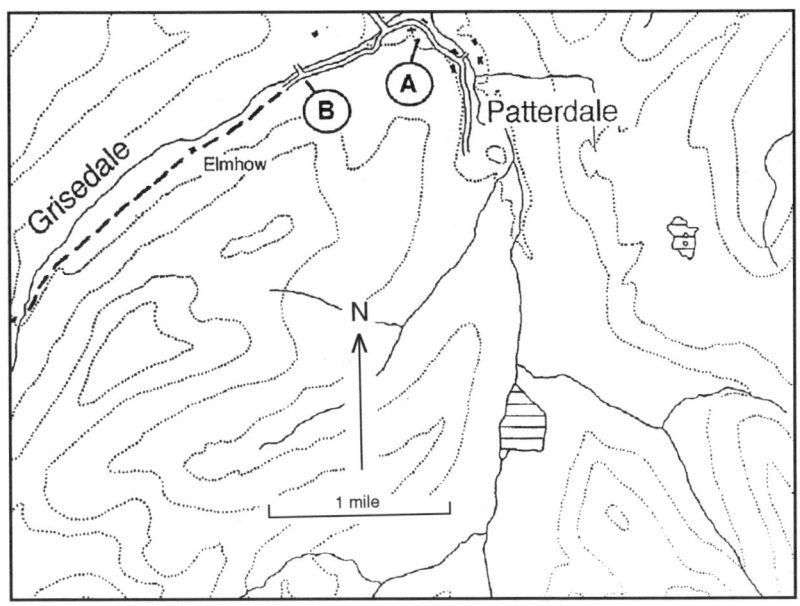

D   This becomes a very distinct path which follows Raise Beck down to Dunmail Raise across which runs the busy A591. Just before reaching the road notice in the final section of the wall to your right, which also leads down to the roadway, a kissing gate. (1 mile)

E   A signpost next to this gate indicates the path leading from it leads to Thirlmere and Keswick. Note that this path follows the outside of the first wall you come to as another signpost verifies. On reaching Birkside Gill follow it downstream to a stone bridge and then follow the trackway leading from the bridge through the conifer woods surrounding Thirlmere. The trackway soon joins the A591. (¾ mile)

F   At this point the A591 forms a junction with a road signposted as leading to Armboth. Follow this road to Dobgill car park. (1 mile)

From here on follow the High Level Route from directional note 6 onwards on pages 36 and 37.

DAY 3 Derwentwater to Ennerdale

	High Route	**Low Route**
Mileage	13 miles	12 miles
Total Feet of Ascent	4,500 feet	2,500 feet
Highest Point	Dale Head	Rigg-Sail Pass
	2,473 feet	1500 feet
Suggested Time	9 hours	7 hours
Starting Point	High Lodore Farm (261 183)	
Finishing Point	Black Sail Youth Hostel (195 124)	

DESCRIPTION

Both the High Level and Low Level Route on this section of the tour have their merits and it is difficult to say which is the best option to take. The High Level Route is a classic Lakeland ridge walk with a number of major 'undulations', the steepest one of which is the ascent from Dale Head Tarn to the top of Dale Head itself which has recently been very usefully cobbled. (And who would ever think walking this path that it was two young German girls, Kerstin Langewiesche and Antje Wiede, who were partly responsible for its construction? For nearly a year in the early nineties they worked for the National Trust as volunteers building paths in the Lake District, receiving nothing in payment but simply for the chance it gave them to improve their English. That they should have done so should not go unrecognised: which is why I here mention these facts.) There are, of course, some very impressive views to be had on this route. The view northwards from the summit of Dale Head along the length of the Newlands valley and on to Skiddaw is particularly noteworthy. But the best view to be had of all, I think, is from the shoulder of High Snockrigg from which point an almost 'aerial' view of Buttermere village is obtainable.

The Low Level Route on the other hand whilst not having, of course, the elevated quality of the High Level Route has perhaps more variety and perhaps also has a more 'explorative' quality to it as well. To begin with it takes in a longer section of the Derwentwater shoreline than does the High

Level Route, and probably the best part of the lake's shoreline at that with fine views towards the mountain of Skiddaw. After that it progresses through Newlands valley: a dale surrounded with an array of shapely peaks. From Newlands it then passes over to Buttermere by way of a pass which is nameless on the map but which I suppose should be called the the Rigg-Sail Pass after the two becks the path follows. This is a classic V-shaped pass with the fells rising steeply either side of the path. As you descend the other side an ever developing and entrancing view of the Buttermere valley unfolds: a sight to evoke memories of childhood fantasies.

From Buttermere village both routes merge and follow an old packhorse route over to the head of Ennerdale. This is a wild valley compared to all the other valleys this tour has yet passed through and, but for Black Sail Hut, devoid of habitation.

LOGISTICS

Accommodation at the head of Ennerdale is limited to either camping or staying at Black Sail Youth Hostel; should neither of these forms of accommodation appeal to you the only other alternative is to stay in Buttermere. If you choose to stay in Buttermere you are pretty much committed then to sticking to the Low Level Route the following day as the addition of the Scarth Gap ascent on to the demands of the next day's High Level Route would make the walking too exhausting to be comfortable – unless that is you decide to curtail the fourth day's journey as well and conclude it in Wasdale rather than Eskdale. Staying over in Wasdale, however, would in turn affect the way you plan your fifth day – as is explained in the Logistics section for Day 4 on page 53.

PUBLIC TRANSPORT (See also page 7)

In 1995 CMS introduced a tourist season bus service from Keswick to Buttermere via the Whinlatter Pass (195 245) and back to Keswick along the B5289 over Honister Pass (225 136) to Grange and then along the western side of Derwentwater. The service runs both clockwise and anti-clockwise. If the same pattern continues in future years it will be possible to journey to Buttermere, if you are not up to walking it for any reason, directly from Grange Bridge (253 174)) which is three quarters of a mile south-west of High Lodore Farm. However doing this would give you some foretaste of the glories of Borrowdale which is best saved for Day 5, so if you have to use public transport to get to Buttermere I would recommend travelling via Whinlatter which would involve first travelling to Keswick. Travelling this way round also gives you the opportunity of viewing Crummock Water and the Vale of Lorton.

The Derwentwater Launch already referred to travels both clockwise and anti-clockwise around the lake calling at five landing stages including Keswick (263 227), Ashness (269 203), Lodore (264 192) High Brandlehow (252 197) and Hawse End ((251 212). It can therefore be used not only as a way of journeying to Keswick but also as a novel way of beginning the High Level Route or the Low Level Route.

ACCOMMODATION (See also page 7)

Buttermere Two hotels, a number of B&Bs and Buttermere Youth Hostel

Head of Ennerdale Black Sail Youth Hostel

CAMPING

The only official campsite on this day's route is in Buttermere village, but there is no problem in camping at the top end of Ennerdale next to the River Liza a few hundred yards south-east of the youth hostel.

PLACES OF SUSTENANCE

Buttermere Both the hotels in the village, The Fish and The Bridge, have public bars which serve bar meals. In addition there is a small farm cafe in the village which in summer sells snacks and cups of tea or coffee.

SHOPS

None! though a few dairy products can be bought from a farm in Buttermere village and Black Sail Youth Hostel has foodstuffs for sale if you are self catering.

EXTRA DAY OPTIONS

From Black Sail Hut a circuit of Hay Stacks (193 132), Green Gable (213 107) and Great Gable (210 103) would be an enjoyable round to accomplish if you planned to stay two successive nights at the hut.

If you decide to curtail Day 3 by concluding it in Buttermere and stop on there an extra night a good 'rest day' option for the intervening day would be to undertake a circuit of Crummock Water calling in at Loweswater on the way which has an excellent pub. A more arduous option, starting from Scale Force (150 170), would be the Buttermere fells: Red Pike (160 154), High Stile (170 148) and High Crag (180 140) and possibly also Hay Stacks (195 132).

DAY 3 Derwentwater to Ennerdale

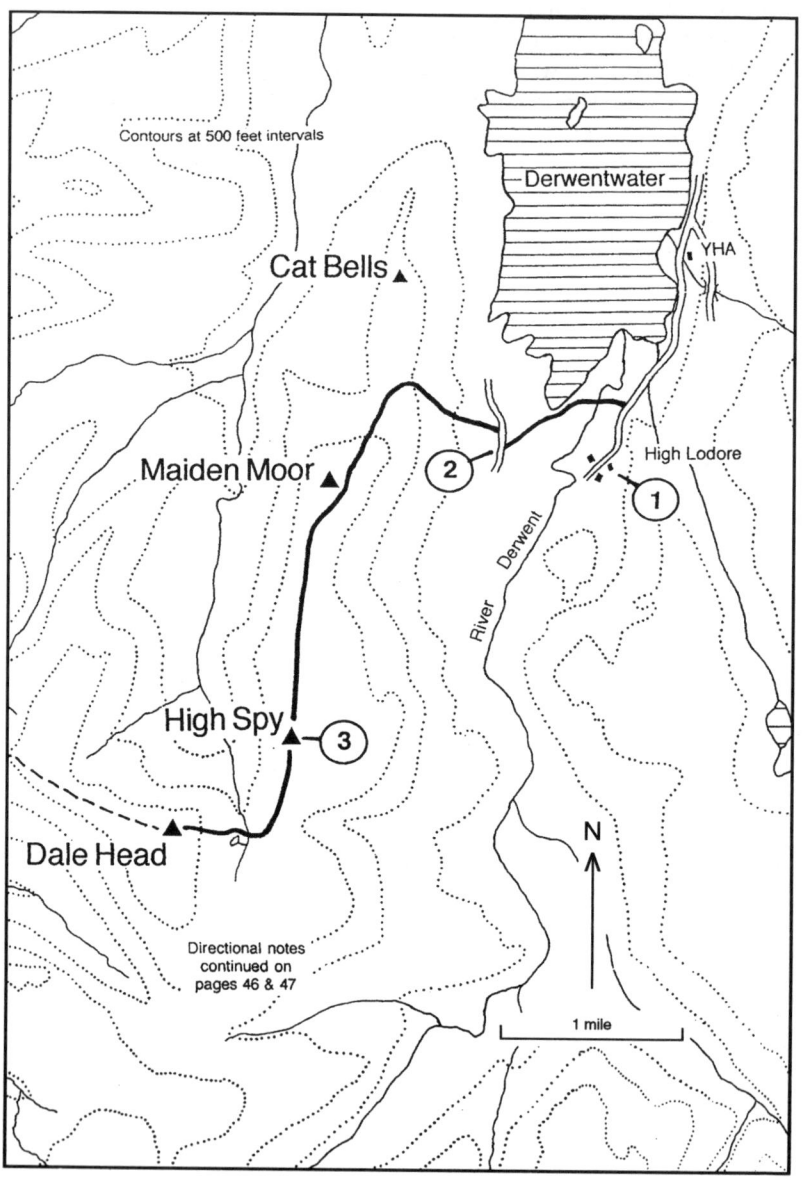

High Level Route

1 Follow the B 5289 northwards. A quarter of a mile along the road a metal signpost points westwards to a broad pathway leading to a bridge spanning the River Derwent. Cross over the bridge and follow the duck boards leading away from it on the other side. After passing through a small gate the duck boards soon discontinue and a path leads from their termination to the southern most tip of the lake. At this point branch off left from the shoreline path on to a path following a line of oak trees. This path eventually leads to the Grange to Portinscale road. (1 ¼ miles)

2 Here turn right. Little more than two hundred yards along this road, on the left-hand side, indicated by a wooden signpost, is the start of two paths. Follow the right-hand broader path (you may in fact in any case fail to notice the left-hand path). Within a few hundred yards this broad trackway branches in two. Take the left-hand branch. After a steep climb the path reaches the gap between Cat Bells and Maiden Moor where it joins a ridge path. Here turn left and follow the ridge path on to Maiden Moor and then on to High Spy. (2 ¾ miles)

3 From High Spy a well worn path descends southwards veering to the right away from the line of the ridge towards a deep cut stream flowing into Newlands valley. The path crosses over the stream and climbs uphill a little to reach Dale Head Tarn. The path passes the right-hand side of the tarn as you reach it, its northern edge, and then pulls steeply uphill to the summit of Dale Head. (1 ¼ miles)

DAY 3 Derwentwater to Ennerdale

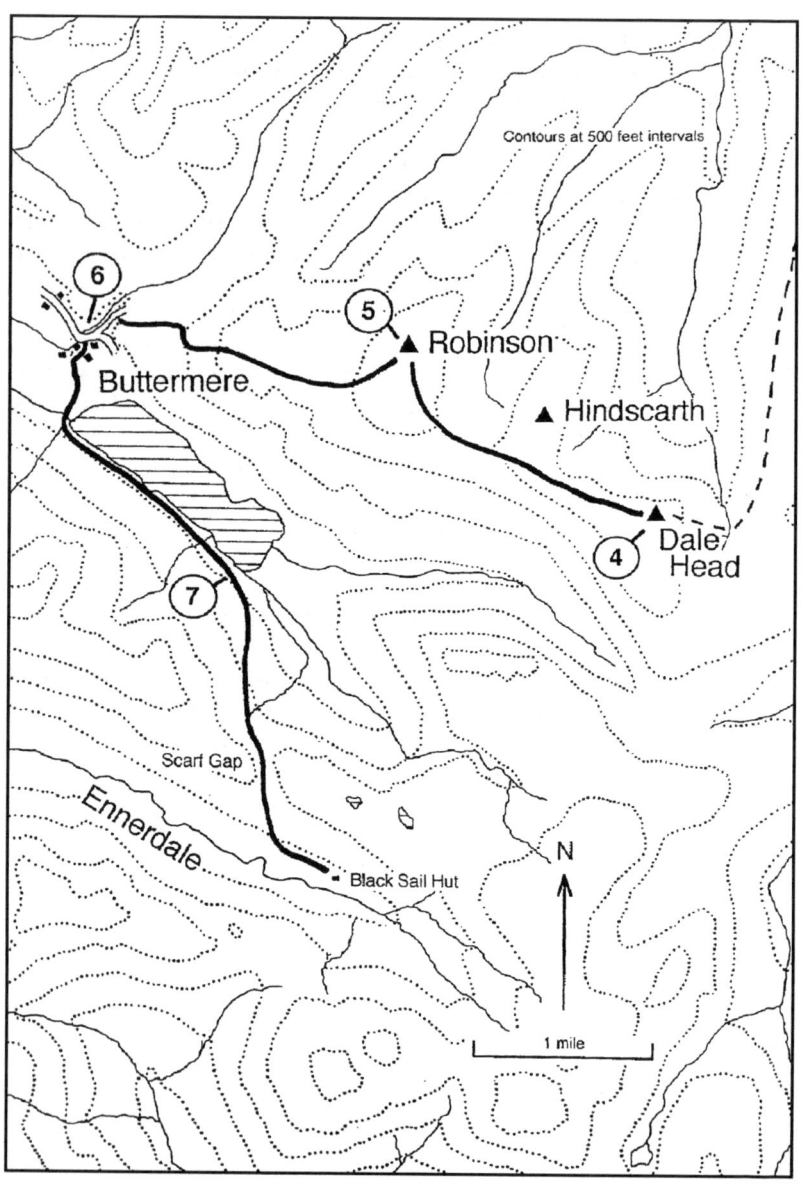

High Level Route

4   From the summit of Dale Head follow the distinct ridge path that leads north-westwards across the shoulder of Hindscarth and then on to the summit of Robinson. (1 ¾ miles)

5   From the top of Robinson head in a south-westerly direction towards a prominent cairn about a hundred yards from the summit. From this cairn a fairly distinct path descends to a flattish stretch of soggy ground called Buttermere Moss which it crosses to a point a few hundred yards north of the top of High Snockrigg. Here it makes a final descent to the village of Buttermere itself. (2 miles)

6   On reaching the Bridge Hotel in the middle of Buttermere village turn left on to the trackway which runs past the gable end of the hotel and then on past the left-hand side of the Fish Hotel which stands behind it. This trackway leads to the western corner of Buttermere lake. From a footbridge spanning the outflow of the lake a path continues along the south-west shoreline of the lake. On nearing the far end of the lake look for a pathway branching off to the right taking a diagonal course across the fellside. (1 ¾ miles)

7   Within a few hundred yards this path joins an old packhorse path which climbs up to the top of Scarth Gap. From the top of the gap the packhorse path then drops down into the valley of Ennerdale on the other side where it joins a broad trackway. Here turn left. Black Sail Hut is a few hundred yards further on. (1 ¾ miles)

DAY 3 Derwentwater to Ennerdale

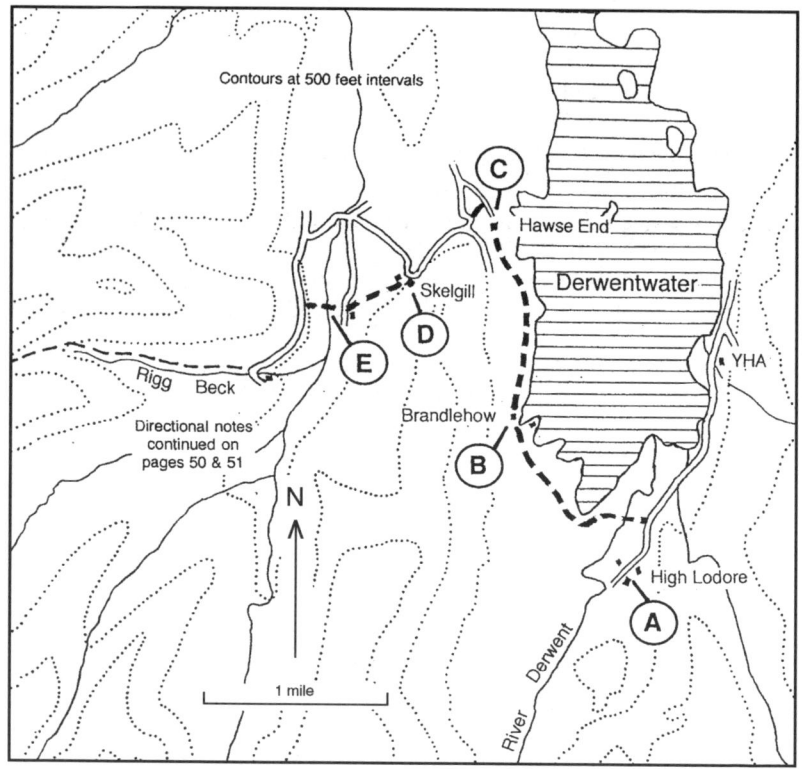

A   Follow the B5289 northwards. A quarter of a mile along the road a metal signpost points westwards to a broad pathway leading to a bridge spanning the River Derwent. On the other side of the bridge the path moves round the southern end of the lake utilising a series of duck boards eventually reaching a surfaced driveway. (1 ¼ miles)

B   Here turn right. Within about a hundred yards the driveway branches in two. Follow the left-hand branch which soon reaches a six bar gate giving access to a footpath following the shore line of the lake. This path eventually reaches the driveway leading to Hawse End Cottage. (1 ¼ miles)

Low Level Route

C   Roughly one hundred yards along this driveway a pathway, signposted as leading to Cat Bells, leads off to the left along the side of a stone wall. Within another hundred yards the path comes to a surfaced roadway. Follow the road uphill across a cattle grid. The road soon makes an hairpin bend at which point another road branches off to the right signposted as leading to Skelgill. On reaching the hamlet of Skelgill the road passes through a gateway and then swings right downhill. Where it swings right again an unsurfaced driveway leads off to the left towards a small farmstead, an almost illegible, moss covered, slate sign nearby indicates it as also being a footpath to Ghyll Bank and Rowling End. (Do not confuse this path with the path starting from the horse trough, slightly higher up the road, which passes the gable end of Skelgill Farm.) (½ mile)

D   The right of way follows the driveway past the farmstead to a five bar gate and stile. Here the path acquires a grassy surface and follows the wire fence to your right. Though not a distinct path its line is well indicated by a series of gates and stiles. Eventually the path reaches another roadway. Here turn left. Within a hundred yards a narrow gate on the right-hand side of the road gives access to a path leading down to a footbridge crossing Newlands Beck. (½ mile)

E   From the footbridge the path continues directly uphill to another gateway where it crosses a driveway to a private house and then veers diagonally left through a spinney of trees to yet another roadway. Here turn left and follow the road south-westwards for about half a mile. Where the road takes a sharp hairpin bend across a stone bridge branching off to the right is the start of a path following the course of Rigg Beck with nothing to indicate where it should lead but just a National Trust sign saying surprisingly "No Unauthorised Vehicles" (½ miles)

DAY 3 Derwentwater to Ennerdale

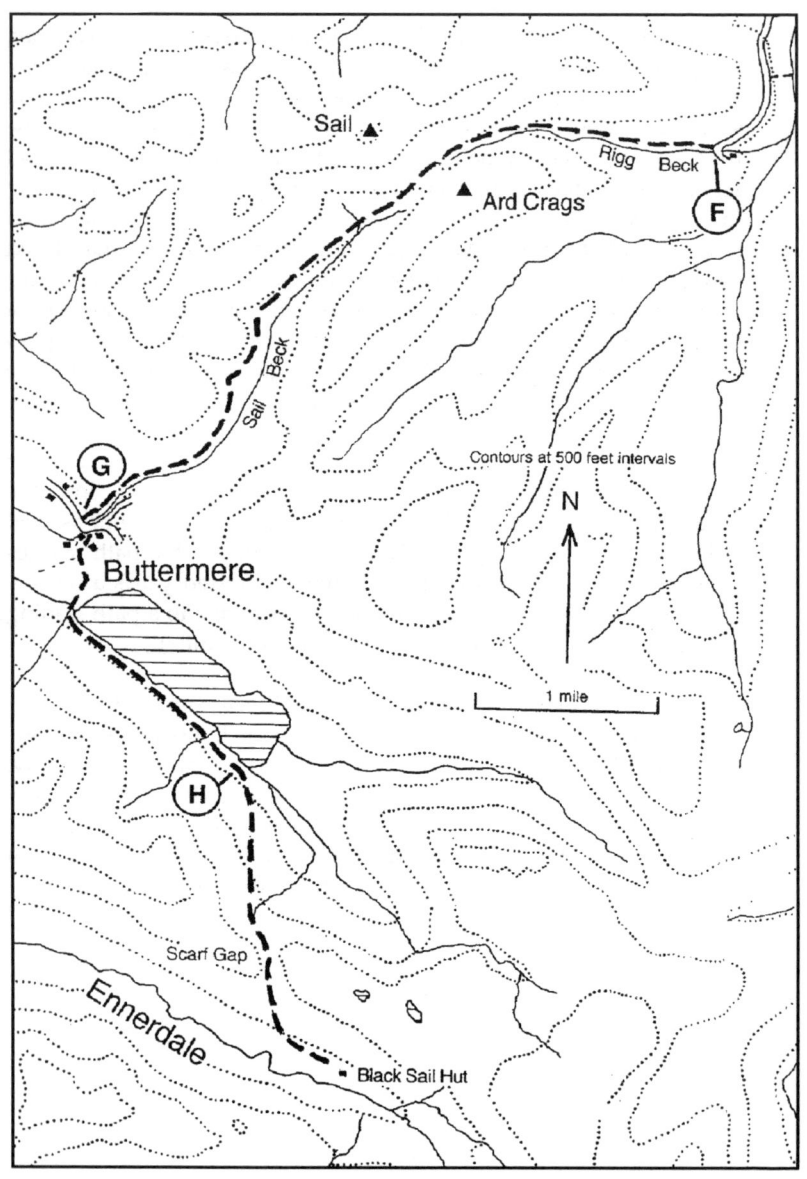

Low Level Route

F Although this path is a fairly broad path to begin with it becomes far narrower further on, even so there is no problem following this path as it crosses the narrow nameless pass between Ard Crags and Sail and then descends along the side of Sail Beck on the other side to the Buttermere valley. On reaching the roadway at the end of the descent turn left to reach the Bridge Hotel. (4 ¾ miles)

G On reaching the Bridge Hotel turn right on to the trackway which runs past the gable end of the hotel and then on past the left-hand side of the Fish Hotel which stands behind it. This trackway leads to the western corner of Buttermere lake. From a footbridge spanning the outflow of the lake a path continues along the south-west shoreline of the lake. On nearing the far end of the lake look for a pathway branching off to the right making a diagonal course across the fellside. (1 ¾ miles)

H Within a few hundred yards the path joins an old packhorse path which climbs up to the top of Scarth Gap. From the top of the gap the packhorse path then drops down to the valley of Ennerdale on the other side where it joins a broad trackway. Here turn left. Black Sail Hut is a few hundred yards further on. (1 ¾ miles)

DAY 4 Ennerdale to Eskdale

	High Route	**Low Route**
Mileage	12 ½ miles	8 miles
Total Feet of Ascent	3,300 feet	1,600 feet
Highest Point.	Pillar	Black Sail Pass
	2,927 feet	1,800 feet
Suggested Time	8 hours	5 hours
Starting Point	Black Sail Youth Hostel (195 124)	
Finishing Point	Boot (176 010)	

DESCRIPTION

The High Level Route this day uses what I think is the most exciting path in the Lake District – the high level route to Pillar Rock. This path was developed by an early rock climbing pioneer called John Tyson Robinson who followed an undulating, shelf like formation across the northern face of Pillar mountain to Pillar Rock (after which the mountain is named) which was then, and still is, a major rock climbing crag. A view of Pillar Rock is obtained once you reach a prominent little knoll at the end of this path atop of which is sited an equally prominent cairn called Robinson's Cairn. The cairn was built in Robinson's memory by the members of the Fell and Rock Climbing Club, of which he had been a member, the year after he died in 1907. Also in his memory, affixed to the crag beneath the cairn, is a beautifully worded copper plaque which every visitor to this place should make a point of reading.

From the cairn there follows a steep climb to the top of Pillar and there afterwards a rugged, airy ridge walk over the rocky tops of Scoat Fell and Red Pike, followed by a descent through the quiet seclusion of the Overbeck valley that gradually opens out to give an impressive view of the sombre waters of Wastwater and the remarkable Screes which hang above it.

By comparison the Low Level Route is some what tamer: but only by comparison. Mosedale, which the route passes through, is an awesome amphitheatre of rocky crags that cannot fail to impress.

From Wasdale Head the two routes converge and cross Burnmoor: a small elevated plateau. Here for the first time on the journey the terrain is open and spacious with long vistas ahead. The route across it follows the course of an old corpse road a bridleway over which in the distant past the deceased of Wasdale were brought to be buried in Eskdale.

Crossing Burnmoor brings you finally to Eskdale a valley dotted with snug, robust farmsteads and copses of pleasing deciduous trees. Above them all stand the sturdy, granite crags of the surrounding fells making this one of the most appealing valleys in the Lake District.

LOGISTICS

The Low Level Route is easy to accomplish but if you follow the day's High Level Route Wasdale may seem the natural place to conclude the day's wanderings rather than pressing on to Eskdale. Adding these final four miles on to following day's itinerary, however, is an even more exhausting prospect. So if you do wish to stay in Wasdale this decision will effectively mean your having to extend the tour by an extra day simply to walk from Wasdale to Eskdale which is by no means a full day's walk. If, however, you decide on staying at the southern end of the Wastwater, which is where Wasdale youth hostel is situated, you could consider journeying to Eskdale by taking in the Whin Rigg (150 030) to Illgill Head (169 049) ridge which then makes the journey to Eskdale a near full day's walk. But no matter how many hours you have to idle in Eskdale there is so much to explore and discover there you are bound to have a full day of interest.

PUBLIC TRANSPORT (See also page 7)

None! It is though possible to reach Eskdale from Buttermere during the tourist season firstly by travelling to Keswick and then on to Whitehaven by bus and then by train to Ravenglass from which in turn you can travel to Eskdale on the Ravenglass to Eskdale Miniature Railway. Obviously this is not a journey to look forward to save for its final section.

ACCOMMODATION (See also page 7)

Wasdale Head (186 088) Two or three farm B&Bs and the Wasdale Head Inn (See under Places of Sustenance)

Nether Wasdale (126 040) B&Bs, two small hotels and Wasdale Youth

Hostel (144 044) which from its dining room windows has an impressive view of the towering Screes across the waters of Wast Water.

Boot (176 010) B&Bs, village inn and Eskdale Youth Hostel (195 010).

CAMPING

There are three official campsites on the actual route: the **Wasdale Head Inn** campsite (186 088), which is very small, and the National Trust campsite at **Wasdale Head** (182 075), which is extremely large but is closed between November and Easter, and a campsite in the village of **Boot** (176 010) which as campsites go is possibly the best in the Lake District. Not on the route but of relevance is a campsite in **Nether Wasdale** (126 040).

The best 'wild' camping site option, which I've often used, is the area around Burnmoor Tarn.

PLACES OF SUSTENANCE

Wasdale Head Inn (186 088) Serves bar meals.

Nether Wasdale (126 040) Two splendid village inns which both serve meals.

Boot (176 010) A good village inn, the Burnmoor Inn, and Brook House a tearoom/ restaurant.

SHOPS

Wasdale Head (186 088) 'The Barn Door' outdoor shop next to the Wasdale Head Inn sells a range of camping supplies including non-perishable foodstuffs and confectioneries.

Boot (176 010) The small P.O. in the village carries a small selection of food specifically for backpackers and newspapers in the summer. A much larger food shop is to be found in Eskdale Green (140 001) two miles down the valley – if you are too weary to walk this distance you might consider using the Ravenglass to Eskdale Miniature Railway.

EXTRA DAY OPTIONS

Eskdale is a glorious valley and there are many places to explore such as Stanley Ghyll (17 99) and Eel Tarn (189 009) which make pleasant saunters, as does a simple walk along the banks of the river Esk itself. Should you wish for a more substantial walk an ascent of Harter Fell (219 997) is recommended. The completely idle however can content themselves with a ride on the 'La'al Ratty'- the Eskdale miniature railway – to explore the unprepossessing coastal village at its terminus and perhaps also nearby Muncaster Castle (103 965).

DAY 4 Ennerdale to Eskdale

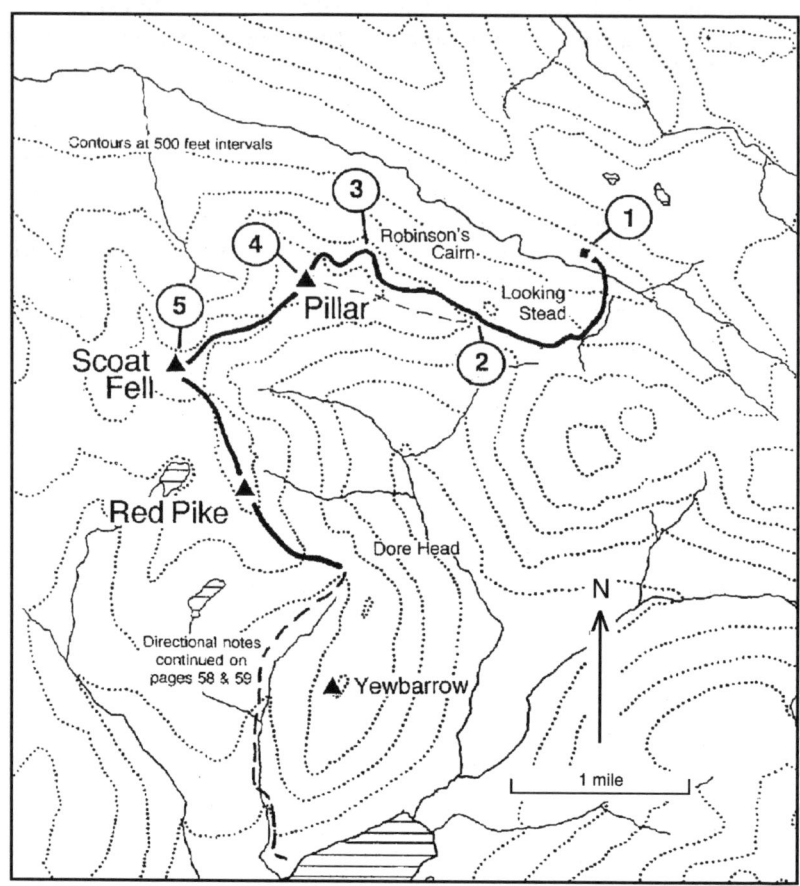

1. From Black Sail Hut walk upstream along the River Liza a few hundred yards to the broad footbridge which spans it. From the bridge a steep path climbs to the top of Black Sail Pass. On reaching the isolated remains of the metal gate on the top of Black Sail Pass turn right towards Pillar following a path which initially follows a line of metal posts. This path leads to a small saddle between Looking Stead, a small rounded hillock to the right of the ridge, and the shoulder of Pillar itself. (1 ¼ miles)

High Level Route

2   From this saddle the path continues along the shoulder ridge of Pillar to the summit of the fell itself. This is the easiest route to the top but a more exciting route is the high level path to Pillar Rock. To locate the somewhat elusive start of this route begin climbing the ridge but only a hundred feet or so. Look carefully at each cairn you come to. From one particular cairn, at the time of writing it is the second cairn, a narrow path leads off to the right. This is the start of the path which descends slightly to begin with and then delicately traverses the northern face of Pillar to Robinson's Cairn. Unfortunately in recent years a confusing alternative path has developed along this route. About a hundred yards from the start the route now branches in two, though this is not immediately noticeable. Try to ensure that you spot this bifurcation and that you take the left-hand, higher, original and better route. (¾ mile)

3   From Robinson's Cairn the path is obvious enough even if the terrain appears a little daunting. The path descends at first and then ascends a scree slope at the top of which it moves right across a tilted slab, called the Shamrock Traverse, bringing you to a point overlooking Pillar Rock. From here the path ascends a steep ridge to the summit of Pillar. (½ mile)

4   From the summit head south-westwards down to Wind Gap and then along the ridge to Scoat Fell, the summit cairn of which is a small pile of stones set on top of a stone wall. (1 mile)

5   From Scoat Fell head south-eastwards to the top of Red Pike. Initially there is no path but a few isolated cairns which pick out a route across a boulder-strewn surface. From Red Pike a distinct path descends to Dore Head. (1 ¾ mile)

DAY 4 Ennerdale to Eskdale

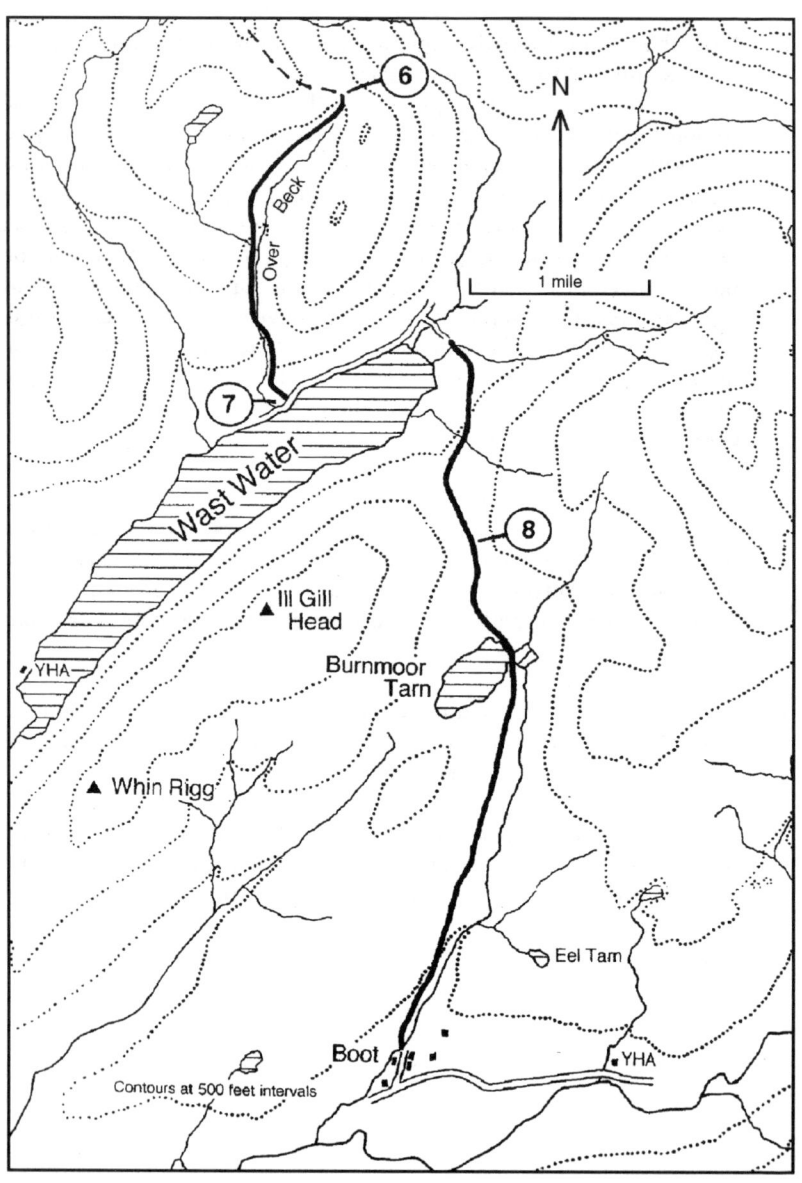

High Level Route

6   From Dore Head move south-westwards into the Overbeck valley keeping to the western side of the stream. Though there is a public right of way marked on the map there is little evidence of a path existing until you come near to Brimfull Beck, the stream flowing from Low Tarn. From this point on you seem assured of an easy path: but not so. The path leads to a wall through which there is no right of way. Here follow the wall downhill to a footbridge crossing Over Beck. The path leading from it on the other side is distinct enough though quite narrow. Soon after it passes through a six bar gate the path cuts across a path that follows the prominent south-western ridge of Yewbarrow and then moves diagonally across the fellside to the lakeshore road of Wast Water. (2 miles)

7   Follow the road to the head of the lake. A quarter of a mile past the lake turn right on to a surfaced trackway signposted as being a footpath leading to Scafell and Boot. After the trackway crosses a broad wooden bridge it branches in two. Bear left. In a short distance this trackway also branches in two. This time bear right on to a bridleway signposted as leading to Eskdale which follows the side of a long wall. After a steady pull of roughly five hundred feet the path branches in two. Follow the well cairned left-hand branch towards the top of the gap between Ill Gill and Scafell. (2 1/4 miles)

8   From the top of the gap the path descends to the outflow of Burnmoor Tarn, after crossing which a path branches right to Burnmoor Lodge, the gaunt isolated building which overlooks the tarn, whilst a few hundred yards further on a path branches left to Eel Tarn. Be sure to ignore these paths (unless you are intending to stay at Eskdale youth hostel in which case the Eel Tarn path provides a more direct route) and keep to the broad path you are on which after a slight ascent descends to the Eskdale valley. (3 miles)

DAY 4 Ennerdale to Eskdale

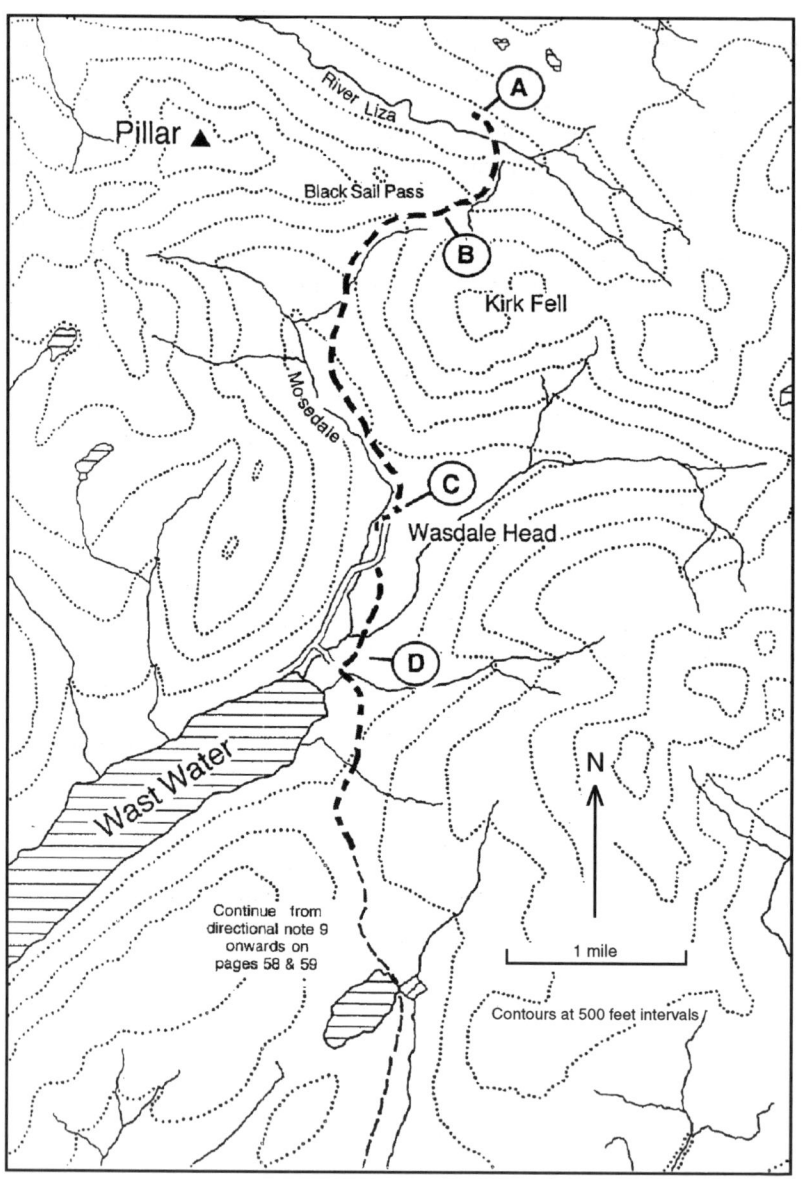

Low Level Route

A From Black Sail Hut follow the path which continues up the valley a distance of a few hundred yards till you come to a broad footbridge which spans the river Liza that runs through the valley. From the bridge a steep path climbs to the top of Black Sail Pass, the gap between Kirk Fell and Pillar. (¾ mile)

B From the top of the pass the path descends to Mosedale and eventually arrives at the Wasdale Head Inn situated at the terminus of the road running through Wasdale. (2 ¼ mile)

C From the inn follow the road down the valley. Roughly a quarter of a mile from the inn leading off to the left through a five bar gate is the start of a signposted bridleway. After fording Lingmell Beck, or crossing its dry bed depending on recent weather conditions, the path runs along the edge of Wasdale camp site. A couple of hundred yards along the edge of the camp site is located a broad kissing gate bearing a sign with the words "Scafells and Eskdale". (1 mile)

D Pass through the kissing gate and turn right. The path soon links up with a broad trackway. Here turn left. Almost immediately the trackway crosses a broad wooden bridge and branches in two. Take the left-hand option. In a short distance this trackway itself branches in two. This time bear right on to a bridleway signposted as leading to Eskdale which follows the side of a long wall. After a steady pull of roughly five hundred feet the path branches in two. Follow the well cairned left-hand branch towards the top of the gap between Ill Gill and Scafell. (1 ¼ mile)

From here onwards follow directional note 8 on pages 58 and 59.

DAY 5 Eskdale to Borrowdale

	High Route	**Low Route**
Mileage	14 miles	13 miles
Total Feet of Ascent	3,500 feet	2,400 feet
Highest Point.	Scafell Pike	Esk Hause
	3,206 feet	2,490 feet
Suggested Time	9 hours	7 hours
Starting Point	Boot (176 010)	
Finishing Point	Rosthwaite (258 146)	

DESCRIPTION

The High Level Route on this fifth day of the walk ascends the highest point in England, Scafell Pike. The route of ascent followed is, in my view, the finest ascent route in the whole Lake District which takes the walker from a pastoral dale through England's most mountainous scenery with several revelations and discoveries on the way. Despite these virtues, however, this route is surprisingly little used. You are likely, therefore, to enjoy a quiet climb and it will come as something of a shock when you reach the top of Scafell Pike to discover so many people crowded there, as inevitably there will be if the day is at all fine.

From the summit the route continues along the highest ridge in England, and also the rockiest, to Esk Hause. From this point looking northwards the full length of Borrowdale can be viewed. It is into this valley the route descends by way of Seathwaite Farm, the wettest inhabited place in England. For half my lifetime it has been my fortune to walk in Borrowdale almost every other day and still I am impressed by its beauty. I think, then, it is well worthy of being considered 'the most beautiful valley in England'.

Though I have included a Low Level alternative, given the rewards of the higher route, and the fact that it needs but little extra effort to accomplish, this lower route should be eschewed unless the cloud base is down to about two and a half thousand feet, in which case there is no point in attempting the higher course.

LOGISTICS

This particular day's walking is quite committing and the 'Low Level Route' hardly less so either, nor is the 'Low Level Route' really a low route in any true sense of the word as it climbs to nearly two and a half thousand feet. You will probably notice as you examine the map, however, there is a slightly easier way of walking to Borrowdale from Eskdale than the 'Low Level Route' I've suggested: that is to walk back over Burnmoor to Wasdale and then over Styhead Pass (219 094) to Borrowdale. Compared to the option I've set out this route is marginally shorter, by about a mile, and requires slightly less climbing, all of about 200 feet. But the highest point on this route, Styhead Pass itself, is much lower than the highest point on the suggested 'Low Level', a difference of 900 feet, and this is the critical difference between the two routes. I have not utilised the Styhead Pass route as my Low Level alternative though because it involves repeating some of the previous day's walking, but should the weather be such as to make the idea of climbing to a height of two and half thousand feet unacceptable then this Styhead Pass route should be borne in mind, even if it does mean retracing some of the steps taken the day before.

PUBLIC TRANSPORT (See also page 7)

To get from Eskdale to Borrowdale involves the following: travelling from Dalegarth Station to Ravenglass on the miniature Ravenglass to Eskdale Railway, then travelling from Ravenglass to Whitehaven on the mainline coastal railway, then travelling from Whitehaven to Keswick on the Whitehaven to Keswick bus (the railway station in Whitehaven and the bus station are only a few hundred yards apart) and then finally travelling from Keswick to Borrowdale on the Borrowdale bus. Such a journey is obviously costly, long and tiring and would also completely destroy the sense of this tour of Lakeland being a walking tour. However if the weather is particularly wretched and you have already prepaid for your accommodation in Borrowdale you may well wish to know of this alternative. If the weather is wretched and you have not prepaid your accommodation in Borrowdale, however, a better plan would be to spend Day 5 sitting tight in Eskdale and then linking on to Day 6 the next day by following the course of the Esk and Lingcove Beck – or more adventurously by passing from Esk Hause (233 081) to Ore Gap (240 072) via Esk Pike (236 074).

ACCOMMODATION (See also page 7)

Borrowdale A valley well endowed with several hotels, B&Bs and also Longthwaite Youth Hostel (255 142)

CAMPING

There are three official campsites in Borrowdale: **Seatoller** (244 136), **Chapel Farm** (257 140) and **Stonethwaite** (267 134).

PLACES OF SUSTENANCE

There are two hotels in Borrowdale which have public bars and which provide bar meals; these are the **Scafell Hotel** in Rosthwaite (258 146) and the **Langstrath Hotel** in Stonethwaite (263 136). In addition there is also the **Yew Tree** in Seatoller (244 138) which provides more up-market meals. For light refreshments there is a small tea room in **Seathwaite** (235 121) and a tea shop in Rosthwaite called the **Flock In** (257 148). Without doubt, though, the best place for tea in Borrowdale is the **Royal Oak** (259 149) in Rosthwaite – though this is only served between 3.30 pm and 5 pm.

SHOPS

Borrowdale Rosthwaite General Stores (259 149) a well stocked shop.

EXTRA DAY OPTIONS

King's How (258 166) Brund Fell (264 162) and Dock Tarn (274 143) can be combined in a single none too strenuous circular walk. A more challenging day's walk can be had either on Glaramara (247 105) combined with Rosthwaite Fell (259 124) or on High White Stones (280 096) via Greenup Edge, or on Great Gable (210 103) via Gillercomb (22 12).

Sprinkling Tarn

DAY 5 Eskdale to Borrowdale

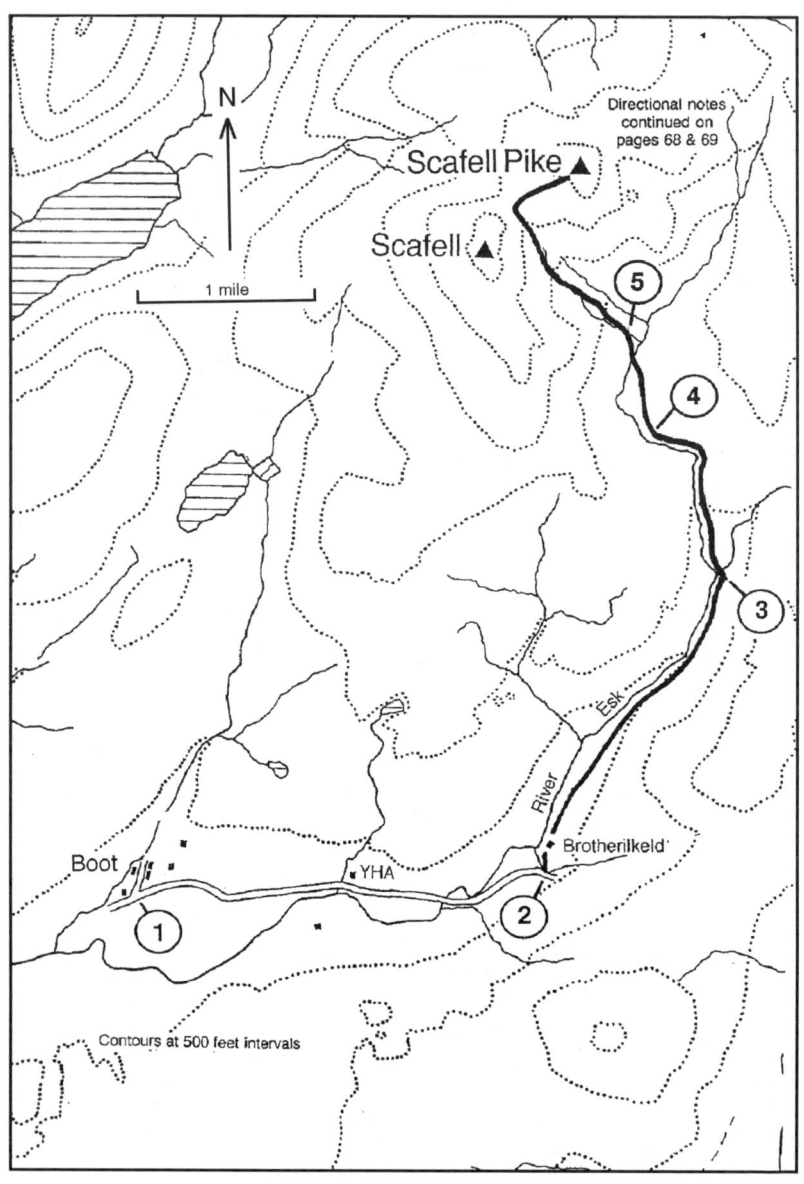

High Level Route

1. From the village of Boot follow the main valley road eastwards to the foot of Honister Pass where is sited an isolated telephone box. (2 ½ miles)

2. Here turn left along the access road to Brotherilkeld Farm. Just before entering the farmyard branch left on to a path which follows the side of the river Esk. After a hundred yards or so the path veers away from the river as it crosses two broad enclosures after which it moves closer to the banks of the river again finally arriving at Lingcove Bridge. (2 miles)

3. Crossing over the bridge the path continues to follow the river Esk but this time at a much steeper angle. Passing through a miniature gorge, however, the terrain dramatically levels and the river takes a large curve westwards. The path continues along the side of the river following its westward course, but in little more than a quarter of a mile the course of the river alters yet again and a wide spacious valley comes into view. (1 mile)

4. Immediately ahead of you is an extensive and impressive rock face called Cam Spout Crags. At the northern end of the crags is a waterfall: Cam Spout, after which the crags are named. Follow a fairly distinctive path which heads to the base of this waterfall, fording the river Esk to do so. (¾ mile)

5. To the right of the waterfall is a steep scramble. This is actually the start of a long, steep, path which leads to Mickledore, the gap between Scafell and Scafell Pike. At the top of this gap turn right and follow a very worn path to the summit of Scafell Pike. (1 ¼ miles)

DAY 5 Eskdale to Borrowdale

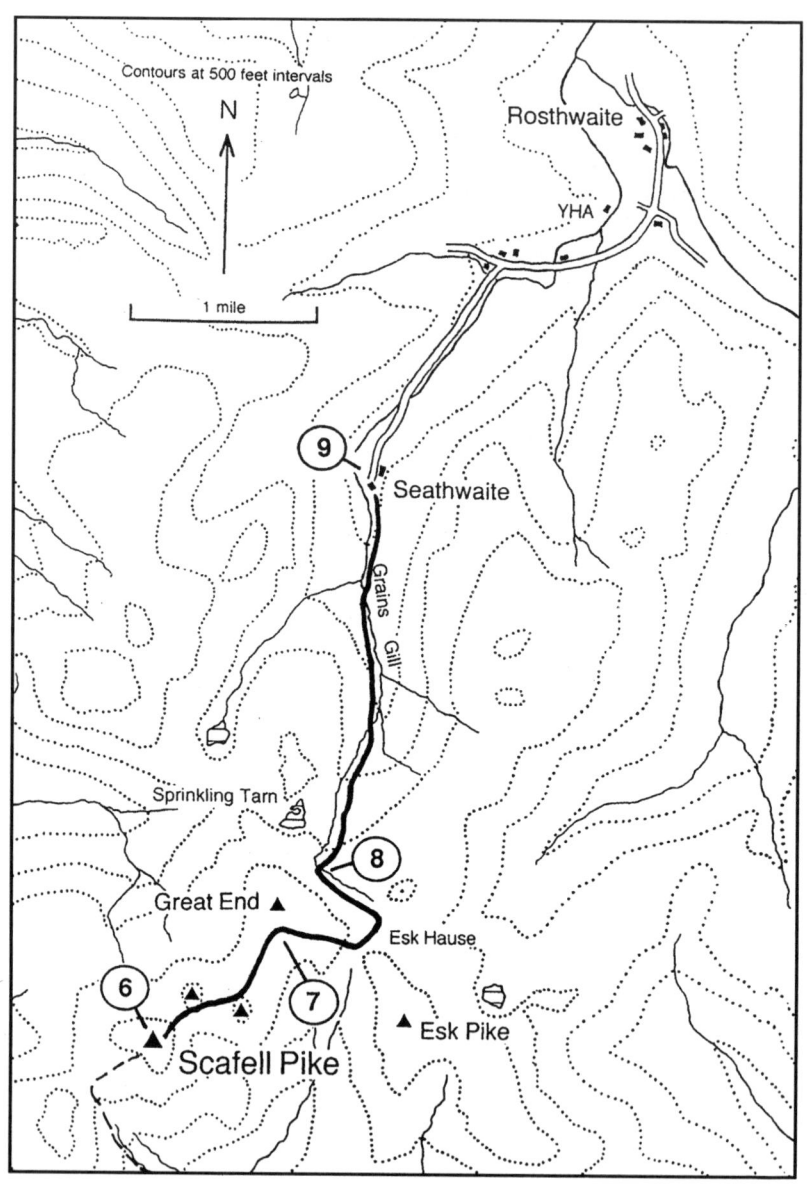

High Level Route

6   From the summit head north-eastwards along a well worn path across some very rough terrain. To begin with there is a fairly sharp drop down to Broad Crag Col and then a climb over Broad Crag itself followed by a shallower descent between Broad Crag and Ill Crag. After crossing over Ill Crag the path drops down to the gap between Ill Crag and Great End. (¾ mile)

7   Here the path swings eastwards to a large flattish area called Esk Hause, the gap between Great End and Esk Pike. As the path approaches the lowest point of this gap notice another path branching to the left curving around the base of Great End. This path links to a path leading to Sprinkling Tarn running parallel to a deep ravine. Follow this path until you reach a distinctive cobbled path leading into the ravine. (1 mile)

8   Emerging out of the ravine the path leads into the valley of Grains Gill which it descends, eventually reaching Stockley Bridge. From the bridge a broad trackway leads northwards to Seathwaite Farm. (2 ¼ miles)

9   From the farm continue along the road which leads to the farm down the valley to the village of Rosthwaite. (2 ½ miles)

DAY 5 Eskdale to Borrowdale

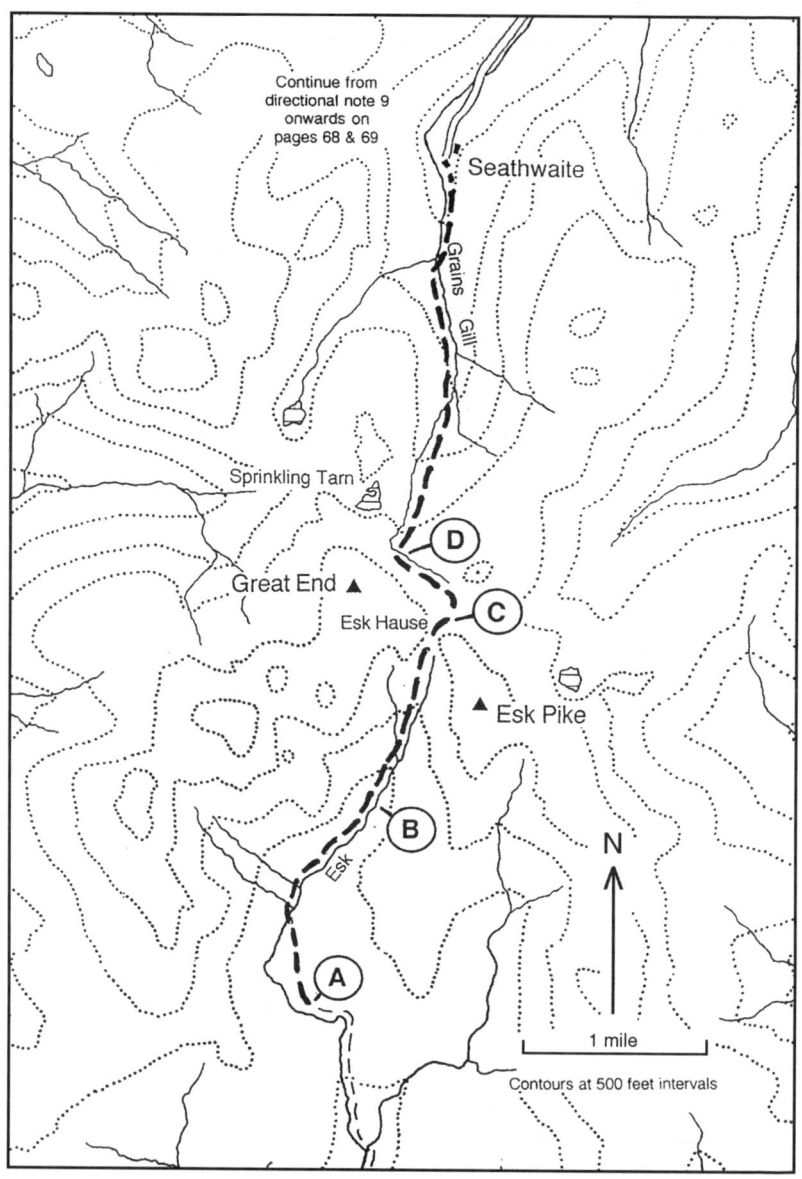

Low Level Route

Follow the High Level Route on pages 66 and 67 to the end of directional note 3, then continue as follows:-

A   At this point the path veers away from the river slightly as it cuts across the valley floor following in part the remains of what was once a stone wall built by the monks of Furness. Once close to the river Esk again, where it becomes particularly broad due to the flatness of the terrain, ford across the river on to its western bank. Here turn right and follow the river upstream once more. Eventually, if not immediately, you should locate a distinct pathway. (½ mile)

B   Passing Dow Crag, one of Lakeland's tallest rock faces, the path branches in two. Follow the right-hand branch (the left-hand branch leads up Little Narrowcove). The path climbs to the head-waters of the river Esk at one point passing through a miniature gorge the narrowness of which restricts progress almost entirely to the course of the stream itself. Passing the last flow of the Esk's head-waters the path is barely perceptible, but now there is only a few feet of ascent left to conquer to gain the top of Esk Hause, the broad gap between Esk Pike and Great End, where a broad stony pathway is met. (1 ¾ miles)

C   Follow the pathway downhill. After passing a stone wind shelter the path intersects with another pathway. Here turn left and follow the new path in a north-westerly direction towards Sprinkling Tarn. In a matter of a few hundred yards the path comes to follow, on your right-hand side, a deep ravine. Follow the side of this ravine until you reach a distinctive cobbled pathway which branches right into the ravine itself. (½ mile)

D   Emerging out of the ravine the path leads into the valley of Grains Gill which it descends to eventually reach Stockley Bridge. From the bridge a broad trackway leads northwards to Seathwaite Farm. (2 ¼ miles)

From here on follow the High Level Route on pages 68 and 69 from directional note 9 onwards.

DAY 6 Borrowdale to Dunnerdale

	High Route	**Low Route**
Mileage	15 ½ miles	15 miles
Total Feet of Ascent	3,200 feet	2,600 feet
Highest Point.	Bow Fell 2,960 feet	Ore Gap 2,600 feet
Suggested Time	9 hours	8 hours
Starting Point	Rosthwaite (258 146)	
Finishing Point	Seathwaite (229 961)	

DESCRIPTION

This day's route is a long trek through a great swathe of wilderness – or at least it seems that way. It parallels quite closely the previous day's walk though for the most part there is little sense of this except on the descent to Green Hole when the lower reaches of the Esk valley might be glimpsed. Apart from that occasion, on the lower route at least, you can easily delude yourself that you might be moving yet still further away from the previous day's starting point.

Whether you choose the high route or the lower route can be decided when you reach Ore Gap. Including a fell top on a day's walk is always satisfying, of course, and the summit of Bowfell is a particularly attractive top that affords fine views of Great Langdale, and from Ore Gap the top of Bowfell requires little extra effort to obtain. The lower route then is included merely to note that it exists should the weather make the reaching of a higher point profitless, or should you feel too fatigued to expend more energy than is absolutely necessary.

Finally the route enters the Duddon valley, the involved topography of which takes a good many hours of exploration to properly comprehend. It is also perhaps the wildest looking inhabited valley in Lakeland due to its numerous rocky outcrops and the wealth of boulders that are strewn over its rugged fields. Being a little cut off from the rest of the Lake District motorists on the whole give it little attention: a circumstance which greatly adds to its appeal.

LOGISTICS

This is a very committing day's walk. As with Day 5 the 'Low Level' route is not that low either, but unlike Day 5 there is no easier alternative. Bad weather, therefore, might well prevent you considering even using this lower route, in which case the only viable option open to you would be to follow the course of Day 6 as far as Stake Pass from whence you can then descend into Great Langdale to follow the course of the valley to the village of Elterwater where you can link up with the final part of Day 7's route. This would of course mean completing a shortened version of the tour in six days rather than seven. However, you can easily fill in a spare day should that be the case, either by perhaps following an easy route to Windermere (see page 95) or tackling a high level walk such as Fairfield (358 115).

I have concluded this particular day's walking at Seathwaite because at the time of writing this is the only place in the Duddon valley where accommodation and sustenance can be found. A more 'natural' place to conclude, in the sense that by the time you reach this point you will probably think you have done enough walking for the day, is Cockley Beck Farm (247 017). In the past this farm has provided accommodation and should it do so again I would suggst concluding the day here and adding the final part of Day 6 on to Day 7 or linking on to Day 7 via an ascent of Grey Friar (260 003). If you are camping, of course, you can emulate this option anyway by camping in Mosedale.

PUBLIC TRANSPORT (See also page 7)

It is possible to journey from Borrowdale to Dunnerdale, though the journey involves using no less than five different bus routes! Borrowdale to Keswick, Keswick to Ambleside, Ambleside to Coniston, Coniston to Broughton-in-Furness and finally Broughton-in-Furness to Seathwaite on a postbus. This is not a journey worth undertaking unless you have pre-booked accommodation in Dunnerdale. In the event of bad weather preventing you from walking on Day 6, therefore, a better option to take would be to sit tight in Borrowdale until the following day and then link on to Day 7 in the manner suggested in the logistic notes.

ACCOMMODATION (See also page 7)

Duddon Valley Limited – a few B&Bs.

CAMPING

There is a small camp site at Turner Hall Farm in **Seathwaite** (232 964). A suitable wild site is likely to be found in Green Hole (23 05) or Mosedale (23 03).

PLACES OF SUSTENANCE

Seathwaite The Newfield Inn (229 961) provides some very fine bar meals.

SHOPS

None! The Newfield Inn however does sell some confectioneries.

EXTRA DAY OPTIONS

A good fell walk is an ascent of Harter Fell (21 99) via Stonythwaite (220 969) and Grassguards (224 982). This is a fine fell from which some remarkable views of the Scafells are obtainable A more leisurely option would be to explore the lower Duddon valley and possibly perhaps crossing over to Broughton Mills (222 906) to visit the Blacksmith's Arms: perhaps the most rustic pub in Lakeland.

The descent route off Bowfell to Three Tarns Pass.

DAY 6 Borrowdale to Dunnerdale

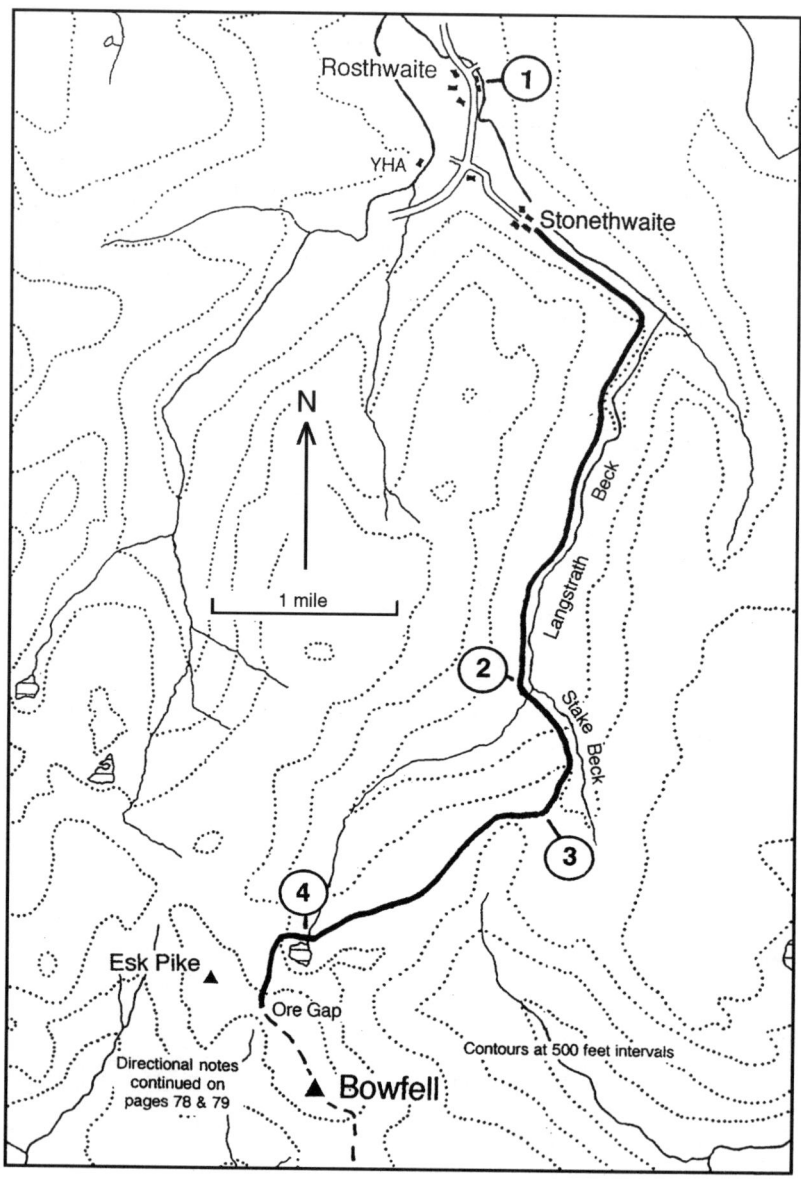

High Level Route

1. From Rosthwaite walk southwards along the main valley road and take the first turn left along a road signposted as leading to Stonethwaite. At the end of the hamlet the route continues as a rough trackway. Three quarters of a mile from Stonethwaite the track turns south into the valley of Langstrath. Just over a mile along the valley the trackway comes to a five bar gate after which it becomes a grassy pathway for a few hundred yards until it reaches rockier ground again and then becomes once more a worn pathway. Just before reaching the confluence of Stake Beck and Langstrath Beck the path reaches a footbridge crossing the latter stream. (4 miles)

2. Cross over the footbridge and bear right towards a large ash tree next to which is a footbridge crossing Stake Beck. Continue along the path leading from the footbridge. This is an old packhorse path which zig-zags its way up the side of Stake Beck to the top of Stake Pass, the top of which is marked with a large cairn. (¾ mile)

3. Ten yards before reaching the top another path branches off to the right which eventually reaches Angle Tarn. (1 ½ miles)

4. Here the path joins a very worn path leading from Langdale to Scafell Pike. At this point turn right and follow the Scafell Pike path. Where the gradient of this path begins to ease a narrower path leads off to the left towards Ore Gap, the col between Esk Pike and Bowfell. (½ mile)

DAY 6 Borrowdale to Dunnerdale

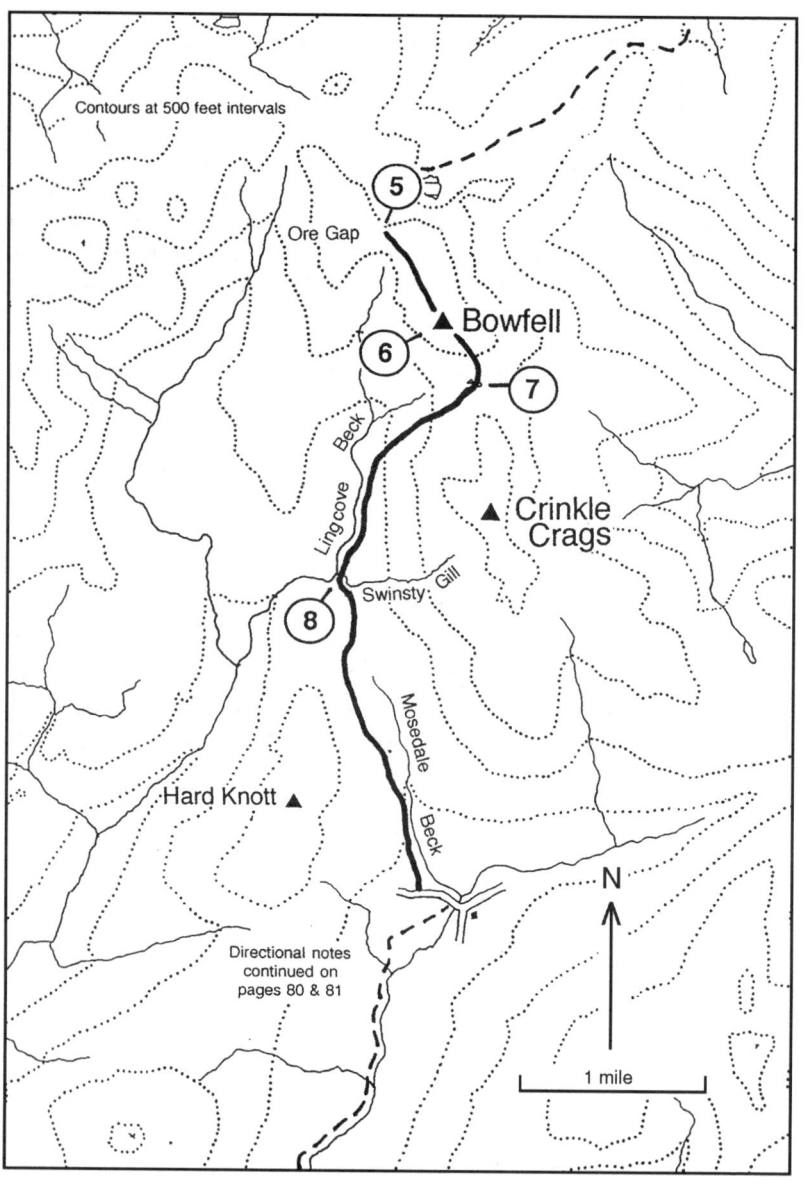

High Level Route

5   Reaching the top of Ore Gap the path comes to a reddish path crossing between Esk Pike and Bowfell. Here turn left and follow this well cairned path to the summit of Bowfell. (½ mile)

6   Continue over the top of Bowfell guided by a series of cairns. At first there is no definite path to follow as the top of the fell is a jumble of rock, but within a short distance, however, the route is more than evident as it becomes one of the most badly eroded paths in the Lake District. At the foot of this descent the path comes to Three Tarns Pass. (½ mile)

7   Walk to the far, southern, side of the first tarn you reach. With your back to the tarn turn immediately right. Within a hundred yards you should locate some very small cairns. These modest cairns mark the start of one of the most unassuming paths in the Lake District. The path's full length is waymarked with a whole series of similar cairns which often have to be relied on to effect the path's successful navigation. The path eventually reaches Lingcove Beck which it then follows on its downhill course. Where the beck takes a large swing westwards another stream, Swinsty Gill, flows in from the left. Following this stream uphill is a very inconspicuous path. (1 ¼ miles)

8   This path soon veers right from Swinsty Gill and leads to the shallow gap between Hard Knott and Crinkle Crags. Crossing this gap the path enters the valley of Mosedale. Veering to the western side of the valley the path proceeds down the length of it. An indistinct and often boggy path to begin with it becomes better the further along it you progress. Eventually the path reaches a surfaced roadway. (1 ¾ mile)

DAY 6 Borrowdale to Dunnerdale

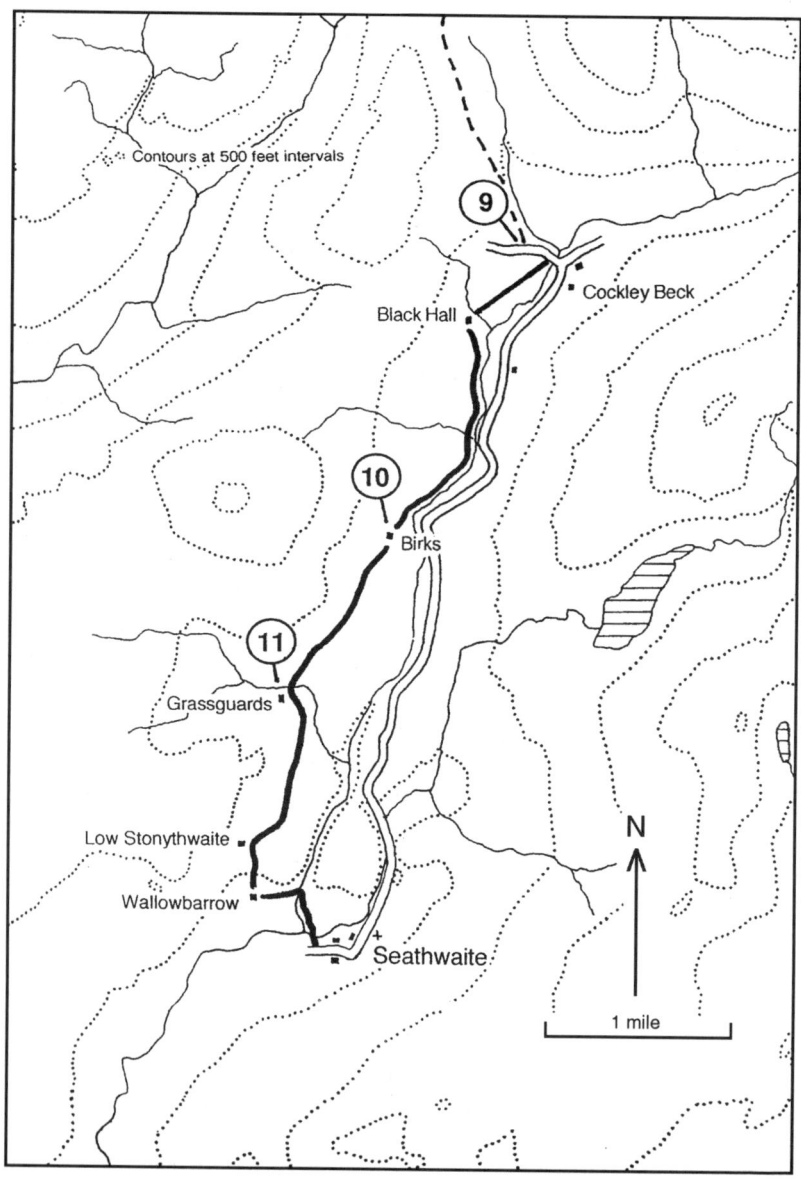

High Level Route

(At this point it is likely that you will feel a little weary in which case the easiest way to reach Seathwaite is simply to follow the Duddon valley road the four and a half miles it takes to get there. There is, however, an interesting bridleway you can follow to reach this same destination and the final directional notes explain how to follow this route.)

9 Here turn left. Just before the road crosses a bridge turn right on to a farm access road leading to Black Hall Farm, signposted as being a public footpath. Passing through the farmyard continue through a wooden five bar gate on to a grassy trackway and through a series of other five bar gates. The trackway eventually becomes a grassy riverside path waymarked with yellow banded posts. After crossing over a forestry road track a few hundred yards further on it joins a much firmer path. This path leads to Birks Farm, now an outdoor centre. (2 ¼ miles)

10 Follow the access road leading uphill from the 'farm' but once over a cattle grid turn immediately left on to a trackway which soon links to a forestry road. Here turn left. Follow the forestry road a hundred yards or so uphill and then veer right on to a rough trackway. After running roughly parallel to the forestry road the trackway cuts across it, the junction is slightly staggered, dips downhill a little and then takes a level course to Grassguards Farm, the final few hundred yards integrating into yet another forestry road. (¾ mile)

11 Follow the trackway running directly in front of the farm which eventually leads to to Low Stonythwaite. A hundred yards before reaching the farm, however, a path leads off to the left making a steep zigzagged descent to Wallowbarrow Farm. From the farm bear left out of the farmyard on to a path signposted as leading to Seathwaite and waymarked with a series of yellow arrows. This leads to a stone bridge crossing the river Duddon. Once over the bridge bear right on to a path following the river downstream. This soon veers left to cross a concrete bridge spanning a tributary of the Duddon in order to reach the main valley road which brings you to Seathwaite. (1 ¾ miles)

DAY 6 Borrowdale to Dunnerdale

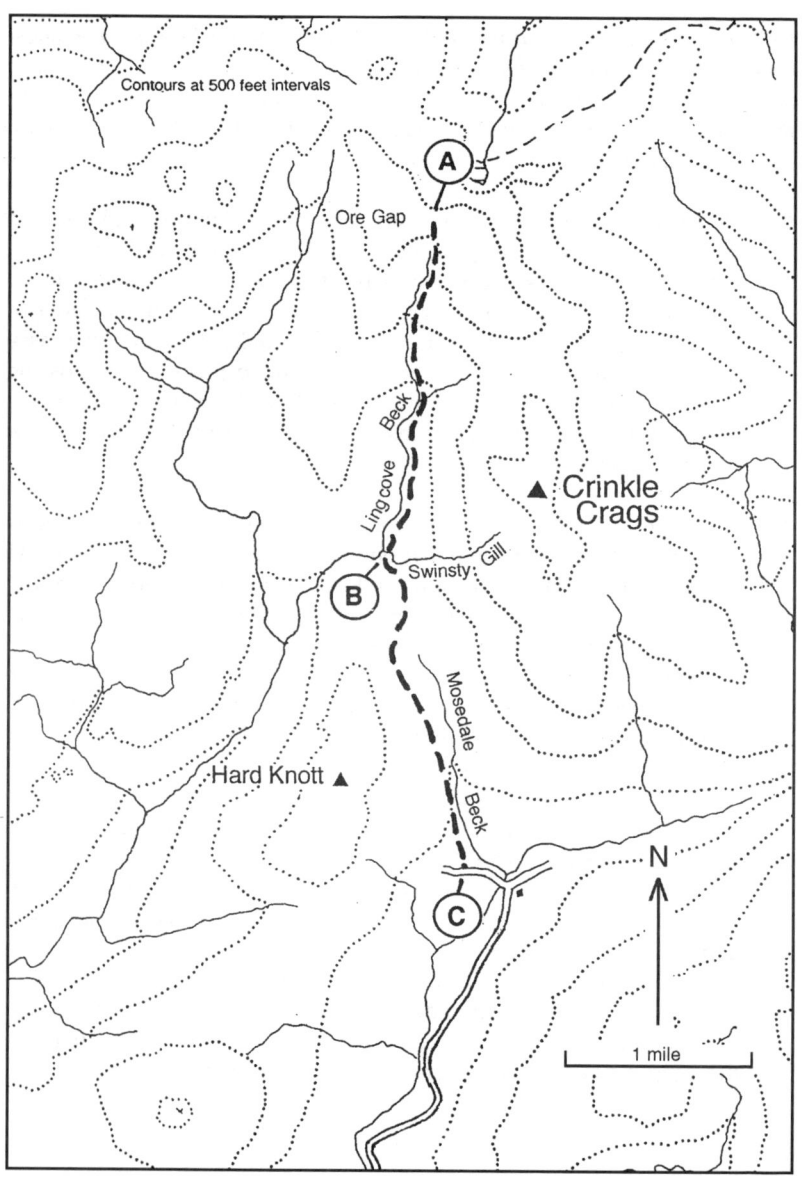

Low Level Route

Follow the High Level Route on pages 76 and 77 to the end of directional note 4 then continue as follows:-

A   Locate a cairn marking the lowest point on the saddle. From this cairn a thin path leads southwards down the other side of the pass following Yeastyrigg Gill. This is a very indistinct path and little better than a sheep trod especially once it reaches level terrain. If you cannot locate the path successfully simply follow the course of the beck, which becomes Lingcove Beck in its lower reaches, as closely as possible. At the confluence of Lingcove Beck and Swinsty Gill note a very faint path veering off uphill to the left initially following the course of Swinsty Gill. (1 ¾ mile)

B   This inconspicuous path soon veers right from Swinsty Gill and leads to the shallow gap between Hard Knott and Crinkle Crags. Crossing this gap the path enters a valley called Mosedale. Veering to the western side of the valley the path proceeds down the length of it. An indistinct and often boggy path to begin with it becomes better the further you progress. Eventually the path reaches a surfaced roadway. (1 ¾ mile)

C   Here turn left. After crossing a bridge a few hundred yards further on turn right on to the Duddon valley road which eventually leads to the hamlet of Seathwaite. (4 ½ miles) *(Alternatively if you wish to keep road walking to a minimum follow the High Level Route on pages 80 and 81 from directional note 9 onwards. This is an interesting route, especially in its later stages, but does require a bit more effort to accomplish, which may not be welcome at the end of a long day.)*

DAY 7 Dunnerdale to Ambleside

	High Route	**Low Route**
Mileage	15 miles	15 miles
Total Feet of Ascent	4,500 feet	3,200 feet
Highest Point	Coniston Old Man 2,631 feet	Walna Scar Pass 1,950 feet
Suggested Time	10 hours	9 hours
Starting Point	Seathwaite (258 146)	
Finishing Point	Ambleside (37 04)	

DESCRIPTION

The final day's High Level Route includes a final ridge walk across what use to be the highest hills in Lancashire until the formation of the county of Cumbria in 1974, followed by a fairly gentle descent to the quiet valley of Little Langdale.

The Low Level Route takes a distinctly different course. Once over Walna Scar it skirts the physical edge of the high Lakeland fells: a conglomeration of rugged, rocky bastions facing a gentler wave of wooded hills across the other side of Coniston lake. Then, after passing through the bustle of Coniston village, it links up with the high route again in Little Langdale by way of the narrow Tilberthwaite valley.

Finally both routes take in the last climb of the walk: the sprawling fell of Loughrigg. A fitting fell to end on for if it were possible to measure in some way the quality of a view against the physical effort needed to obtain it there is little doubt that Loughrigg would score highest. From the top of this modest top in every direction there are magnificent views. Looking to the north-west there is the Vale of Grasmere, to the west there is the splendour of the Langdale fells, to the south-west the Coniston fells, to the south-east the long length of Windermere lake to gaze on, to the east Froswick and the southern end of the High Street range are visible and to the north rises the the fells of the Fairfield Horseshoe. All of these fells the course of this tour has either crossed or wandered close by. Should the reader of these lines have followed this course in some way then the summit of Loughrigg is a fitting place on which to bid one's valediction to the Lakeland fells.

LOGISTICS

Although Day 7 concludes in Ambleside, if you have to wait until the next day before commencing your journey home you might like to consider terminating the day in Elterwater which is a much quieter place than Ambleside and therefore more in keeping with the ambiance of the rest of the walk. The wander over Loughrigg to Ambleside the next morning should take little more than two hours to accomplish which should leave you with almost a full day in which to complete your homeward journey.

PUBLIC TRANSPORT (See also page 7)

It is possible to journey from Seathwaite to Ambleside first by travelling to Broughton-in-Furness by post bus, thence from Broughton-in-Furness to Coniston by a more conventional bus service and thence from Coniston to Ambleside on another bus service. As this is the concluding day of the tour however there is little point in making this journey unless you have pre-booked accommodation in Ambleside, or as the initial stage of your journey homewards. If the latter reason is your motivation then it might better suit your purpose to find your way to the nearest railway station which in this instance is Foxfield Station (209 855) roughly a mile and a quarter south of Broughton in Furness. This seven to eight mile journey you could walk in even the bleakest of weather (the route via Broughton Mills (222 905) is particularly interesting) or you could do the best part of it using the post bus service already referred to. Foxfield Station is on the Cumbrian coastal line along which trains travel either to Lancaster or Carlisle.

Should you wish to curtail the day's walking for any reason then it is relevant to know that there is also bus service from Elterwater to Ambleside, whilst on the Low Level Route the final eight miles or so can be avoided by using the Coniston to Ambleside bus service.

ACCOMMODATION (See also page 7)

Ambleside Every type of accommodation exists here in abundance including Ambleside Youth Hostel (377 031).

Elterwater A number of B&Bs, hotels and two! youth hostels: Elterwater (327 046) and High Close (338 052).

CAMPING

Low Wray National Trust campsite 2 miles south of Ambleside adjacent to the western shore of lake Windermere. (372 016)

PLACES OF SUSTENANCE

Coniston Several cafes and pubs.

Little Langdale Three Shires Inn (315 034) a range of refreshments.

Elterwater The Britannia Inn (327 046) a wide range of refreshments.

Ambleside A plethora of options.

SHOPS

Coniston Several.

Elterwater Has a good village store.

Ambleside Several, the nicest of which is Lucy's on Church Street.

The Walna Scar Road above Coniston

DAY 7 Dunnerdale to Ambleside

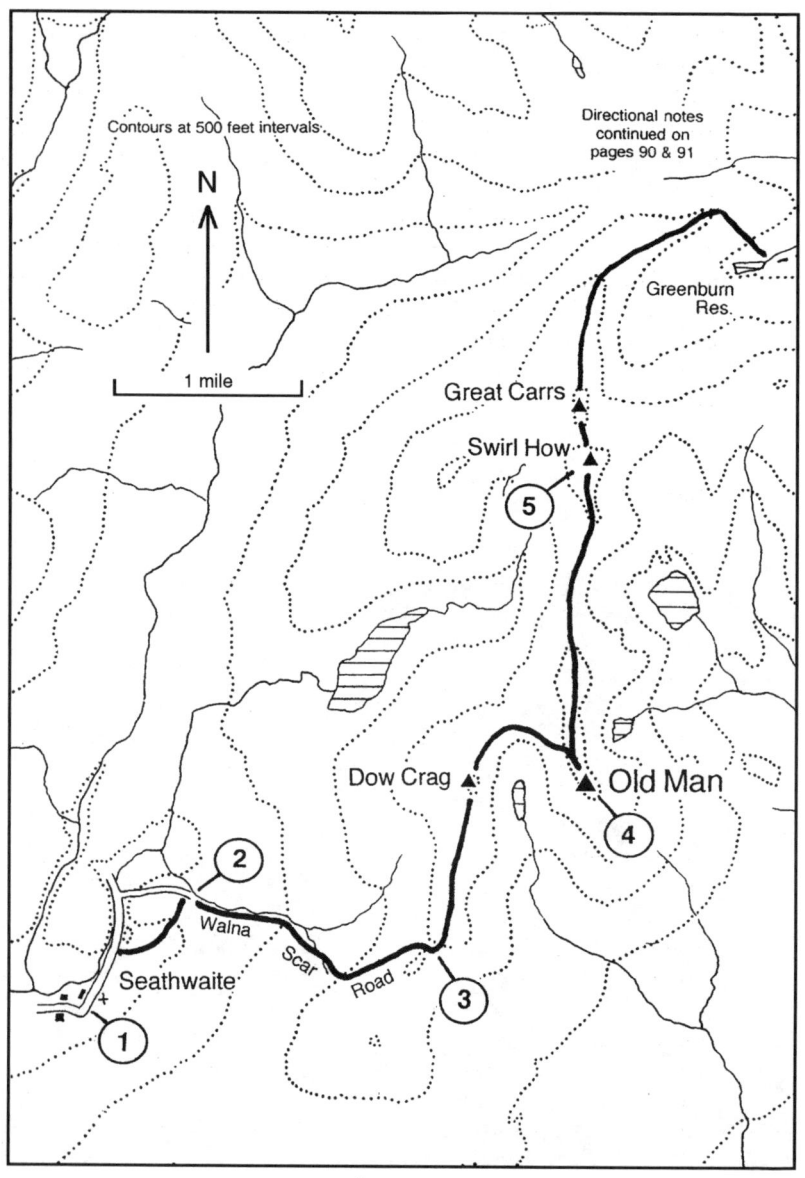

High Level Route

1. Walk northwards along the Duddon valley road. Within half a mile of the Newfield Inn turn right on to the access road leading to Turner Hall Farm. A hundred yards or so along this access road branch left, through a wooden gate, on to another access road leading to High Moss, which in the space of a few yards becomes a rough trackway waymarked with yellow arrows. Reaching High Moss the right of way continues round the left-hand side of the building's garages and then up to and through a wooden gate from which it continues in the direction of an isolated barn. Just before reaching the barn the path comes to a surfaced road. Here turn right. A few hundred yards along this road a wooden signpost points to a rough trackway leading off to the right. The sign indicates that the track is a public bridleway leading to Walna Scar. (1 mile)

2. This is the Walna Scar Road which takes a long steady pull to a shallow col between Walna Scar itself and Brown Pike. (1 ½ miles)

3. From the top of the Walna Scar Road a very worn path leads off to the left following the ridge over Brown Pike, Buck Pike and on to Dow Crag. From Dow Crag a very worn path descends down to Goat's Hawse and then climbs up to Coniston Old Man. (1 ¾ miles)

4. From the top of Coniston Old Man walk back along the path you arrived on but notice a few hundred yards from the top a ridge path branching off to the right which eventually leads to Swirl How. (1 ¾ miles)

5. From Swirl How the ridge path moves on to Great Carrs and then makes a long curving descent towards Little Langdale, the path becoming increasingly grassier the further you descend. At approximately eighteen hundred feet a path branches off the ridge path to the left and descends to the top of Wrynose Pass: be sure to ignore this path. Half a mile or so further on, at roughly thirteen hundred feet, the ridge becomes almost level. At this point veer right down to Greenburn Beck which emanates from a small reservoir. Beginning from some old abandoned mine working, a quarter of a mile east of the reservoir, is the start of a rough trackway. (2 ¼ miles)

DAY 7 Dunnerdale to Ambleside

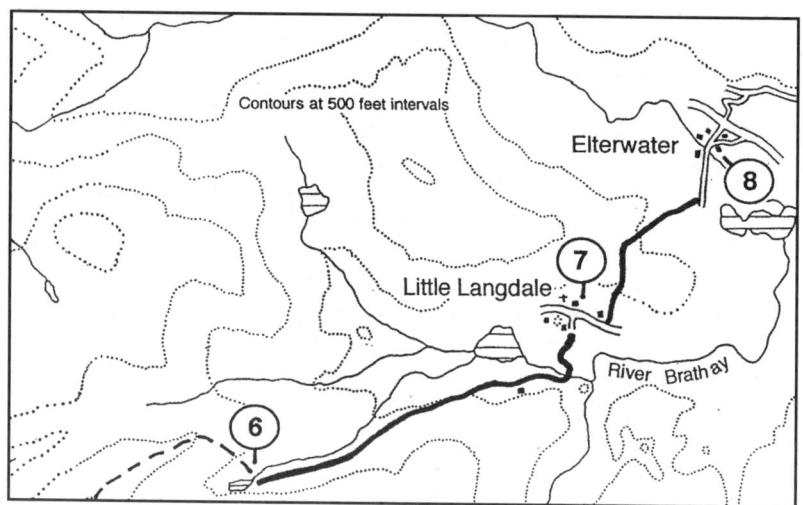

6   Continue along this trackway. Soon after merging with another trackway it branches in two. Follow the left-hand branch towards a group of cottages. Almost half a mile past the cottages the trackway comes to a broad footbridge spanning the River Brathay. Cross the footbridge and continue along the enclosed trackway on the other side to the surfaced road running through Little Langdale. (2 miles)

7   Here turn right. Follow the road but a few hundred yards to the start of a signposted footpath on the left-hand side of the road which initially passes through Wilson's Place Farm. After pulling uphill a couple of hundred feet the path comes to a broad trackway. Here turn right and follow the trackway downhill. On reaching a roadway turn left. Elterwater village is a few hundred yards ahead. (1 1/4 miles)

8   From the centre of Elterwater follow the road signposted as leading to Great Langdale and Grasmere. Within a few hundred yards the road comes to a cross roads. Continue straight ahead on to the road signposted as leading to Grasmere. When, within a few hundred yards, the road comes to a T junction turn right. After passing High Close youth hostel the road soon comes to yet another junction. (1 mile)

High Level Route

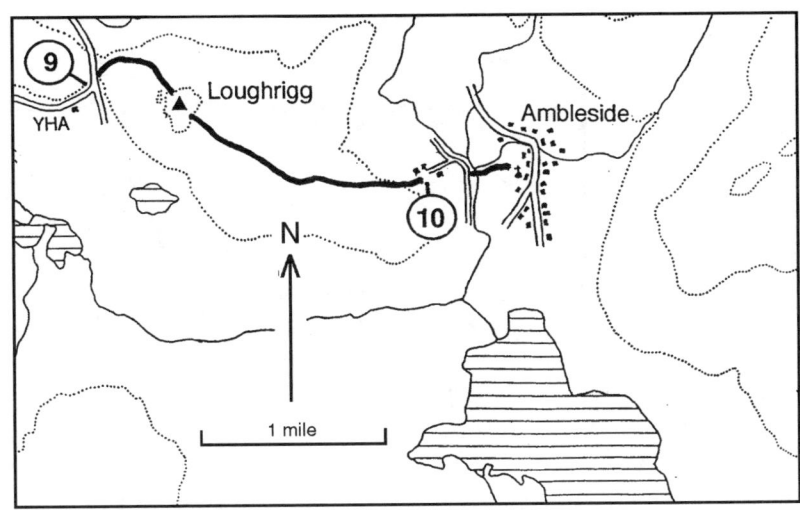

9   Directly across the road is a six bar gate giving access to a broad trackway. Continue on this trackway. After passing through a five bar gate the track reduces to a narrower pathway. Within another fifty yards a distinct path branches off to the right climbing steeply uphill. This path leads to the top of Loughrigg. From the summit of Loughrigg continue downhill the other side of the fell in the same direction in which you approached the summit. Although there are several pathways criss-crossing this rambling fell by keeping to the broadest option possible you should have no difficulty navigating your way towards Ambleside. Passing through a gateway the path gains an increased distinctiveness and beyond a second gate soon becomes a trackway leading to Brow Head. (2 miles)

10 Passing through the hamlet of Brow Head the trackway acquires a tarmacadamed surface and soon joins a narrow roadway. Here turn right. Within 50 yards, on the left-hand side of the road, is a stone footbridge spanning the river Rothay. Two paths lead from the other side of the bridge. Follow the right-hand path through a small park to the centre of Ambleside. (¾ mile)

DAY 7 Dunnerdale to Ambleside

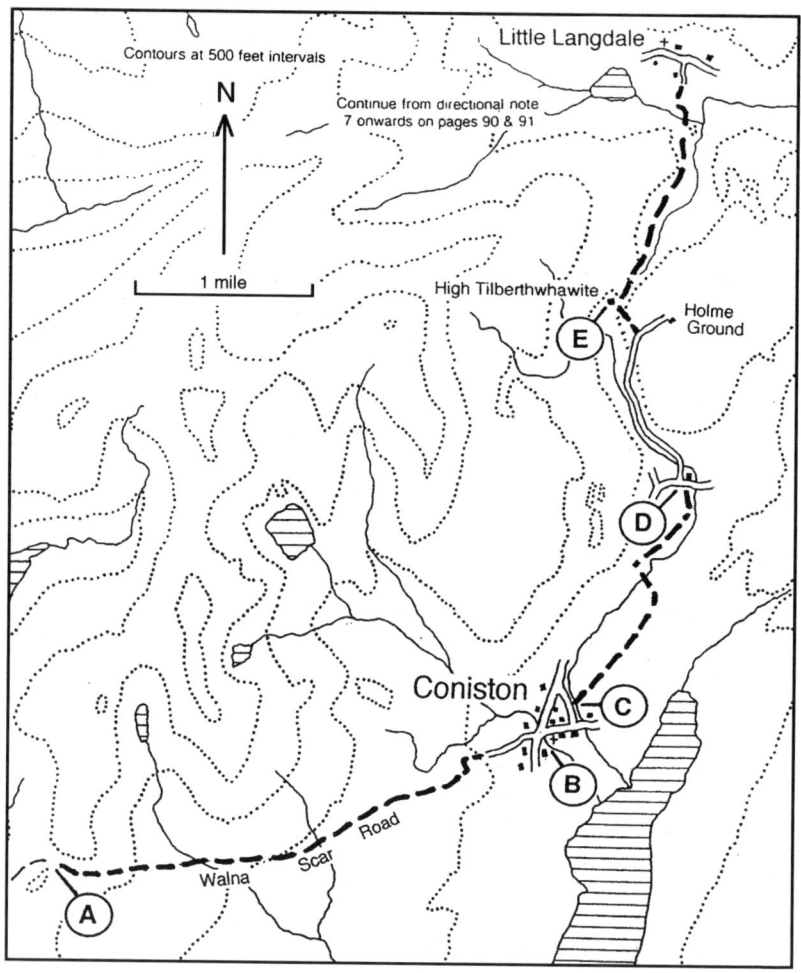

Follow the High Level Route on pages 88 and 89 to the end of directional note 2 then continue as follows:-

A   From the top of the Walna Scar Pass continue along the Walna Scar Road down the other side of the pass to Coniston village. (3 miles)

Low Level Route

B From the centre of the village continue along the road running past the church: the B5285. Four hundred yards along this road, just before the road crosses a bridge, take a left-hand turn on to a road signposted as leading to Ambleside. Follow the road as far as a junior school where a signposted footpath, on the right-hand side of the road, leads off to the right across a small stone bridge spanning Yewdale Beck. (¼ mile)

C Once across the bridge the right of way follows the beck a few yards upstream and then veers off to the right. This distinct path crosses over a small hillock on the descent side of which the path is waymarked with a series of yellow arrows. Eventually the path reaches a rough trackway. Here turn left. After crossing a stone bridge bear right on to a trackway which passes the front of three cottages and then leads to a six bar gate. From here on the right of way continues forward as a pathway in a fairly direct line through a series of gates until it reaches the terminus of a trackway which leads to the main A 593. (1 ½ miles)

D On reaching the main road turn left. After following the road a hundred yards turn right on to a roadway signposted as leading to Hodge Close. About a mile along this road, just after Holme Ground Farm comes into view, a trackway leads off to the left signposted as being a public footpath. (Do not confuse this trackway with another trackway which veers off to the left a hundred yards beforehand but which is not signposted). The trackway leads to the roadway leading to High Tilberthwaite Farm. (1 ¼ miles)

E Here turn right and enter the farmyard. Two trackways exit from the far side of the yard. Follow the right-hand, lower, track which eventually comes to the River Brathay spanning which is a broad wooden footbridge. Cross over the footbridge and continue along the enclosed trackway on the other side to the surfaced road running through Little Langdale. (1 ½ miles)

From here on follow the High Level Route on pages 90 and 91 from directional note 7 onwards.

Extending the Tour

The original conception I had for this tour was that of a near complete circuit ending at Windermere; a railhead. However the final two days of this 'circuit' lacked the 'freshness' of the proceeding days as they came close to covering the same ground that had already been covered. As an alternative I planned a final day's walk from Elterwater to Windermere which I walked twice, once in pouring rain and once in sunshine. Though it was a pleasant enough ramble it did not match up to the quality of the rest of the tour. The true essence of Lakeland I thought was absent, apart that is for the section crossing Loughrigg Fell which I therefore included in Day 7.

Whilst I decided not to include either of these conclusions they may be of interest to users of this guide attracted to the idea of making the tour the near complete circuit I originally had in mind. In case this is so here in outline are the ideas I had:-

Two Day Extension

ELTERWATER TO HARTSOP

HIGH LEVEL OPTION (10 miles, 3,300 feet of ascent, 7 hours.)

Elterwater – Loughrigg Terrace (34 05) – Rydal (36 06) – Heron Pike (35 08) – Fairfield (359 118) – Hart Crag (369 112) – Dovedale (38 11) – Hartsop village 40 13).

LOW LEVEL OPTION (10 miles, 2,500 feet of ascent, 6 hours)

Elterwater to Ambleside follow directional notes 8 to 10 for Day 7. Then from Ambleside to Hartsop via Scandale and Scandale Pass (38 09).

SUSTENANCE

Sykeside campsite next to Brother's Water (402 119) has a good shop and a bar which serves bar meals and is open to people not stopping on the campsite. Next to the campsite, and now under the same ownership, is the Brothers' Water Inn which also serves meals.

ACCOMMODATION

Possible B&Bs in Hartsop village otherwise Patterdale. Nearest youth hostel Patterdale. Sykeside campsite also has a bunkhouse accommodation.

TRANSPORT

The bus from Hartsop to Windermere currently only runs during the height of summer, otherwise nearest bus pick up point Patterdale for buses to Penrith.

HARTSOP TO WINDERMERE (or STAVELEY)

HIGH LEVEL OPTION (11 miles, 2,500 feet of ascent, 7 hours)

Hartsop village to Threshthwaite Mouth (42 10) via Pasture Beck – Thornthwaite Crag (432 100) – Ill Bell (436 077) – Yoke (438 068) – Garburn Pass (43 04).

Here go either left for Kentmere and thence Staveley or right for Dubbs Reservoir – Orrest Head (413 993) for a final panoramic view of the fells – Windermere.

LOW LEVEL OPTION (9 ½ miles, 2,200 feet of ascent, 6 hours)

Hartsop village to Threshthwaite Mouth (42 10) via Pasture Beck – Troutbeck Park Farm (420 057) via Trout Beck – Long Green Head (421 042) – Far Orrest (412 007) – Orrest Head (413 993) – Windermere.

ACCOMMODATION & SUSTENANCE etc.

Windermere: ample. For Staveley see notes for Day 1. Both places have railway stations, of course, and Windermere is a pick up point for National Express coaches.

One Day Extension

ELTERWATER TO WINDERMERE (8 miles, 2,000 feet of ascent, 5 hours)

Follow directional notes 8 to 10 for Day 7 to Ambleside. Thence: Jenkins Crag (384 029) – High Skelghyll (390 029) – Troutbeck (407 026) – Town End (406 020) – Far Orrest (412 007) – Orrest Head (413 993) – Windermere.

ACCOMMODATION & SUSTENANCE etc. As above.

An t-údar ar a chéad thuras go Ceanter na Loch – tuirseach, caite amach! An buachaill bocht!